AUTHOR STYLIST GUIDE

Own Your Greatness, Get Visible, and Share Your Message

Author Stylist

GUIDE

Own Your Greatness, Get Visible,
and Share Your Message

JENNIFER MILIUS

AUTHOR STYLIST GUIDE: OWN YOUR GREATNESS,
GET VISIBLE, AND SHARE YOUR MESSAGE

By Jennifer Milius

Edited by: Meg Welch Dendler, Serenity Mountain Publishing
Published by: Jennifer Milius, Inc., Chesapeake, Virginia
Cover design and interior formatting by: Hancock Media, LLC

©2023 Jennifer Milius
ISBNs:
979-8-9895037-0-4 (paperback)
979-8-9895037-1-1 (ebook)

DEDICATION

To Mom and Dad:
Thank you for encouraging my light to shine.

TABLE OF CONTENTS

INTRODUCTION

Hi, my fellow author and creative! I'm so glad you're here.

It took stamina and courage for you to reach the point where you hit publish and got your book and message out into the world. And although there are many books in the marketplace, I know your book was given to you for a reason. Whether it's an epic fantasy tale, a children's story, a prescriptive nonfiction, a memoir, or something in between, I believe the people who need to read your book and hear your message the most are waiting for you.

As a multi-genre author and developmental editor, I know firsthand the courage it takes to share your work and message with someone else, whether it's one person, a small group, or the public at large. When I left my 20-year corporate career one month before my first book released, I knew I was headed toward my North Star. When *Einstein and the Leaf* released in September 2014, I used my event management and booth attendant skills to host my first book signing. Since then, I have hosted or participated in over 150 book signings, including booths at multi-day expos. When I think about how I got started with speaking engagements in my business, it was because I was approached and asked. I said "yes" to attending, then figured everything out along the way.

Now, just because I jumped in doesn't mean I wasn't scared. I was, but I was way more excited about what was possible. It was as though I held fear's hand, and we did it together.

This book is my way to hold your hand so you say "yes" to your next podcast interview, book signing, or speaking engagement and have what you need to make it a success. You might be curious about the name Author Stylist. It's not about how to find events or appearances or how to figure out your specific style, like a professional in the fashion, makeup, or hair industry. Author Stylist is my phrase and service focused on helping you—a fellow creative and possible introvert—bring out your inner greatness so you become comfortable using your voice, sharing your message, and being visible.

My intention with the *Author Stylist Guide* is to provide baby steps as you prepare for, attend, and wrap up any book signing, podcast interview, or other type of speaking engagement, such as a workshop, school visit, or keynote. Writing your book did not happen all in one sitting. It happened with each word you typed. Each page you created. Each rewrite you did to get it ready. And you have taken another step by realizing that getting visible is necessary in order for your book and message to reach your ideal readers and audience.

To get the most out of this book, treat it like your back pocket coach, planner, and sounding board as you say "yes" to new appearances, whether they are online or in person. You will find stories, guidance, and checklists to not only remind you that you have what it takes, but you will discover the details you need to get started and refine each time. The reflection questions at the end of each chapter were designed to help you self-assess and take steps to the next big event for you.

This book was created out of love and a desire to see you succeed, so make it work for you. Now, this may go against the grain; however, I believe when you love a book, you make it your own. Write in it. Fold page corners. Add tabs and stickies throughout so you can quickly find what you need.

When you are tapping into your unique energy and willingly standing apart from the crowd to shine your greatness, you provide the best catalyst for your story. Your message will make the impact you want it to have because you are owning it. Each opportunity you take is a new level opening up because it will require a little more from you than the previous one. This is what

I mean by *the next big event for you*. And what's more, I know you can handle your next appearance or event, and the next one, and the next one after that simply because you picked up this book. I believe there's only one *you* with your strengths, gifts, personality, and experiences, and you were given your message and story because you are the right messenger for it.

Let's get started!

CHAPTER 1
What Is Your Why?

To have a strong event, you need a strong foundation. When you think about the appearance or event you want to do, it needs to tie back to your vision and goals for your business. To do this, it's important to be clear what your *why* is.

- Why did you write your book?
- Why did you take it a step further and hit publish?
- Why do you want to serve this audience or group of readers?
- Why is your message needed now?

And even if you didn't start out with the intent to run a business, the fact that you are reading this book shows you are stepping more into your role as business owner and leader. Being an author and selling your books is a business. So, why did you create this business?

Before we keep going, take a few minutes to pause and see what answers come to you with each of the above questions. Grab your favorite journal to write down your answers. As you see what you have on your page, do you smile? Do you feel excited to follow your path and discover where it takes you, even if you're nervous?

Let's shift for a moment from why to *whom*. Whom do you want to serve? Whether it's through writing your book or through a guest appearance or speaking engagement, there is an audience you really want to reach. Let's take a few minutes and get to know them.

- How do they *feel* before they either read your book or attend your event?
- How do you *want* them to feel as a result of working with you or experiencing an event with you?
- What does your reader or attendee gain?
- Are there benefits that extend past themselves (i.e., to their family or team)?
- What do those individuals gain?

The more details you can write out, the clearer this person and audience becomes and the easier you'll be able to connect with them on a deeper level so your event is something they want to attend.

Let's take this a step further and craft a vision statement for your business. A vision statement acts as a compass or filter for decision-making so resulting actions move you closer to the desired end state. It's clear, concise, and meaningful to you. It's something you can wholeheartedly get behind and enthusiastically share with others.

To get the creative juices flowing, set a timer for twenty seconds and write down key words or phrases you want associated with you when people think of your books, your business, or your message. Do this a few times to see what comes up because with each round you'll dig deeper, and the juicy stuff will show up.

As you look over what you've brainstormed, are any of them speaking to you? Do you smile when your eyes see a certain word or phrase? Do your eyes keep going back to certain ones? Each time something draws your attention in this way, put a star by it.

Next, go back to what you wrote for your *why* and write a sentence or two blending your why with the starred words or phrases. And in true writing fashion, this first pass is the most challenging because you're going from nothing to something. Yet this first pass, just like when you're writing a book, does not have to be perfect. It just has to be on the page.

Once you have something on your page, you have a great starting point for your vision statement. In fact, say your vision statement out loud a few times and notice how you feel.

You should feel excited about it *and* about making strides to reach it. Your vision statement is a clear way to remember and share your why. It's also language you can use as you promote your business on your website, in social media, in media kits, on business cards, and so on. As you go about refining it, be sure to choose strong words that stretch your imagination and potential. Your vision statement is about where you're going and why it matters, and because it's meaningful and important to you, it will require more from you.

And that's a good thing.

You will rise to the occasion, and your confidence will grow even more as you lead your business, speak at your next engagement, or host your next event. Your readers or attendees will know you are focused on serving them, will want what you're offering, and will be excited for the transformations they will experience.

Reflection Questions

- Are you clear on whom you want your books, business, and message to serve?

- Does your current vision statement feel aligned with whom you want to serve, where you are, and where you're going?

- Does your current vision statement feel aligned with how you want your business to be perceived?

- What new things have you learned about the audience you want to serve that will help you create a deeper connection with them?

- How have you incorporated your vision statement into your website, social media, media kit, or other methods for promoting your business?

CHAPTER 2

Remember Who You Are

As you continue participating in different appearance opportunities—whether it's a local book signing, a keynote speaking engagement, or something in between—success starts by remembering your value and taking care of you.

I sincerely believe:

- There's only one you with your strengths, gifts, personality, and experiences.
- You were given your message and story because you are the right messenger to tell it.
- The people who need to hear your message the most are waiting for you.

Even though I said this in the Introduction, it bears repeating: When you are tapping into your unique energy and willingly standing apart to shine your greatness, you provide the best catalyst for your story. Your message will make the impact you want it to have because you are owning it.

Yet, as much as I believe this is true and possible for you, it is more important you believe this.

Your guests and readers attend your appearances for a reason. They want a solution, whether it is to purchase your book as the perfect gift for someone or experience a deeper transformation so they grow. They see you and your business as part of their solution, which means the more you get comfortable owning your message and standing apart from the crowd, the better you will be able to serve your people.

You are a generous and talented person, and you are reading this book because you want to create a memorable experience and powerfully serve your audience.

To do this well, you must strike a balance between giving and receiving. When you put other people ahead of your needs and forget to take care of yourself, you won't have as much to give. Even though you'll do your best because this is who you are, imagine what that looks like if you focus on some time for you first.

Take a few minutes and think about the last week. Jot down a few notes of what you did to celebrate and take care of you. Do you have a favorite tea you love to drink? Did you make it? If you did make it, did you savor each sip and stay present in the moment, rather than mindlessly drinking it? Did you make nutritious meals and enjoy them? Did you spend time with people you love and stay present the whole time? Did you get restorative sleep? Did you go on a walk or to the gym to nurture your body? If your faith is important to you, did you pray, meditate, or attend services? The things that nurture your soul, your body, and your mind are so important.

Although those activities can be easily overlooked or pushed down on the list, they're vital because when you do little things for yourself that feel restorative and confidence-boosting, you will exude confidence.

When you think about this upcoming appearance and all the effort required to do your best, setting boundaries is necessary. This might look like protecting your time and energy before the event or interview and allowing some downtime afterward. If it's an all-day event or a multi-day event, what are some easy, healthy meals you can prepare ahead of time so when the event is done you can replenish your energy? If you live with other people who could help in some way, ask them for what you need. Setting boundaries can also look like saying "yes" to appearance opportunities that genuinely light you up, as well as trusting your little voice inside when it lacks enthusiasm for an appearance and saying "no," even if it's a "no for now." When you keep your focus on the priorities that are important to you, you're actually saying "yes" to them, even when you said "no" to other opportunities.

Part of remembering your value and taking care of you is letting go of the things that need to go, and at the right time, with grace. Although it may sound easy, it can be difficult when those things once held a special place in your heart.

Just like when you were writing your book, you reached a point where you needed to start refining and rewriting to strengthen the story or message. It involved eliminating paragraphs, characters, and subplots, all to create a better book. It's the same principle here. Yet now what you might let go of is the need to know all of the questions in advance from a podcast host in order to shine during your interview. Or perhaps you let go of second-guessing your intuition when it says "yes" to your "next big thing" and trust you're on the right path.

Whatever is coming up for you, imagine what it would feel like if you said "yes" to what you want more of and let go of the doubt. This is important because you are essentially asking your audience or readers to do that too. When they attend your book signing, you might like them to let go of money in exchange for what your book will give them. When they attend a speaking engagement or workshop, you might like them to let go and shift their perceptions to the new idea you are proposing. When they hear you in an interview, you might like them to listen, which might mean they stop doing something else in order to pay attention. As you continue to grow as a writer and as a business owner, you are letting go of the older versions of yourself. Thank the previous versions for the lessons and gifts they provided, and trust you are at this new level because you're ready.

Reflection Questions

- Whom do you want your audience to become?
- Whom do you need to become for your audience?
- What do you need to let go of to help you rise to the next level?
- What do you need to allow more time to do?
- Are your boundaries supporting the changes you're making?

CHAPTER 3

Micro Decisions
and What You Know

Back in my corporate days, I was the project manager for dozens of trade shows, as well as attending hundreds of shows.

The first few times I was a booth attendant, I wasn't completely sure what to do except be present, be open, and be engaged. Those three things were exactly what was required. Sure, I had to set up the booth display for the conference I was attending, but the company's marketing team put together the booth boxes I had to unpack and arrange. They provided all the things I needed to set up our space at the event, and all I had to do was unpack, set up, and show up each day to man the booth.

For three years, I was the primary conference representative for my company, and there were six invaluable tips I learned and still apply today.

1. Dress for the occasion, and use the style tips in Chapter 8.

2. Remember, you are "on the job" the moment you leave your hotel room (or car) until you return to your hotel room or are driving home.

3. Stay hydrated; it helps to keep your energy high and throat clear.

4. Use slow times to handle restroom or snack breaks.

5. Consider the clothes to wear on set up and break-down days. For me, that meant pants.

6. Smile and stay present.

When I left that company, I thought I'd left my booth attendant days behind me too. Hah! That was so not the case. Yet instead of being the booth attendant for my new company, I held several positions requiring me to create and execute recognition events, as well as open houses and trade shows within the company. In a nutshell, my job was about building bridges between employee engagement efforts and the company's bigger vision. Sometimes it would look like writing keynote communications for senior leadership, and sometimes it was hearing the vision and creating an event showcasing how the company was achieving those goals.

The first time I was tasked to project manage one of these events felt like a baptism by fire. It was one of the most prestigious events at the company, and I had no idea how it worked behind the scenes. I only knew what the rest of our 20,000 employees knew—who won and what for.

As I learned the ropes for pulling this kind of an event together, I realized I had done this before on much smaller scales during my undergraduate internship and with various parties I hosted at home. Sure, there were a lot of things I didn't know, but I stayed focused on wanting to create the best experience possible for all of the attendees, especially the winners. I wanted them to feel valued and treasured. I wanted everyone who attended to enjoy themselves, and that goodness would have a ripple effect after they left the event. I created a project plan to get clear on what was needed, by when. If the task was delegated, who had the action?

This plan was imperfect, but as I learned more, I refined it so each step got a little bit easier. Then, when I was tasked to run oversight on this same event the following year, as well as create and execute several smaller ones, I had a better grasp of what was required and was able to improve with each one.

Fast forward to January 2014, and I'm in my last corporate job, project managing the last event I'll run as a corporate employee. One of the keys to this event being a success for the company was the booth attendants owning their authority. This event was showcasing a new direction for the company, and most of my booth attendants were introverts, which meant manning a booth was way out of their comfort zones. I didn't blame them. In fact, as an introvert myself, I understand the energy exchange needed to be able to proactively run a booth for eight to ten hours. On top of that, when it's not something you're used to doing, it's easy to get in your head and question if you'll do a good job.

Here's the thing: You are the best person to run the booth or table when you are the subject matter expert. In the case of this corporate event, each one of my booth attendants were those experts. They knew the material they were presenting hands down, and they were excited about the new direction. But they were uncomfortable with all the attention a booth attendant would get. To help them become more comfortable, here's what I advised:

- Treat this day like a really important job interview, so bring your best self.
- Focus on the person in front of you at your booth.
- Focus on delivering incredible value to the person with whom you are engaging.
- Smile.
- Remember, you are the best person to represent your table or booth.
- Trust that the people who approach your table or booth actually want to hear what you have to say.
- Protect your time and energy before the event, and allow yourself downtime after the event.

Let me break this down some more.

It may seem odd to view manning a booth on the same playing field as an important job interview, but to me, it is. You are putting yourself out there for someone else to discern if you're the right fit for the solution they need. So, if it means you need to pick out your clothes and press them the night before, go for it. If it means you want to make sure you hit the gym or go for a run the morning of, go for it. If it means you stop by your favorite coffee shop and get your favorite pick-me-up to drink on the way over to the event, do it. And if it means you play certain songs—while singing at the top of your lungs—in the car as you drive over, then set up your playlist the moment you start your vehicle.

There are many ways to shift your energy from being nervous to being excited, so even if the above ideas are not your cup of tea, no problem. Do what works for you. When you treat the day of this event as something important, you'll show up with the right mindset, and that energy will come through.

All of those are things that I do, except for the gym or run part. Instead, I take my time in the morning, savor my tea, say some prayers, and allow more space to get ready. In fact, the day of my first book signing, I did all of these, even though the event was in the late afternoon. I knew it was going to be a busy day with the book signing, then a private celebration with family and close friends.

My first book signing was one month after I left corporate and started my business, and since September 2014, I've hosted or participated in over 150 book signings, including booths at multi-day expos. Yet I go back to the same guiding steps I learned from my first experience with manning a booth and later coaching others to own their space as a booth attendant.

With these examples, the main actions that happened were micro decisions. Each small step was courageous and continually built upon to grow confidence.

Confidence is developed because you were willing to do something that felt courageous to you. It's about you taking the first step, and the next and the next, even when you may not be taking a direct path from A to Z, but more like A to D to B to K to P to R to Q to L to S to Y to Z.

Confidence is built when you are working through the discomfort of having taken that leap of faith, or a single scary step, or even a series of steps. It's also waiting patiently and peacefully when there is nothing further for you to do in the moment.

That is how courage and confidence work.

Confidence comes *after* you courageously take action, no matter how big the step is.

Yes, there are plenty of times when you're getting ready to do something really big and you know it, but it also takes a lot of seemingly little steps or decisions that get you there and keep you going afterward.

Sometimes, the bigger hurdle is not to secure the event or appearance or interview, but rather to execute it. To show up and to really put yourself out there. It does take courage to pitch, to ask various businesses to host a book signing, ask media specialists for school visits, or do a speaking engagement or workshop and leverage your book as part of it. However, once the other person says "yes" and your event is moving to the next stage, there is a new level of pressure because it is a new level for you. Even if you have done hundreds of events, each one is a little different and will require something more from you.

Make the decision to:

- Go into each event with an open mind.
- Focus on being of service.
- Trust you will do your best at that event.

When you view the opportunity through the lens of possibility, you put fear in its place so your joy, enthusiasm, and passion will be in the driver's seat. Even if the fear might be there, it's in the back seat, taking a nap.

Reflection Questions

- What are your accomplishments thus far? What micro decisions helped you achieve them?
- What do you do to shift your energy and focus to possibility and joy when you're nervous?
- What comes up for you when you think about saying "yes" to opportunities that are "big" for you?
- What are things you can do to stay open to "big" opportunities?

CHAPTER 4
Reframing Sales and Money

I started my entrepreneurial journey in high school with babysitting. There were several families in our neighborhood I would babysit for on a regular basis. If you think about it, this meant I had steady, pipeline work and started honing my time management skills. I made money, and it did not feel like selling. It was simply an exchange of goods, and I enjoyed providing something of value and being paid for it.

This changed when I first got into the workforce and was introduced to sales. It felt awkward and icky—focused only on what and how much you could get, not what you could give.

And I deeply desired to be of service.

Years later, when I was approached by one of my directors during my consulting stint to move to the sales team, I shied away from it. My consulting role was in line with what I wanted to provide: service, encouragement, strategies, and support.

As I progressed in the corporate world and at a different company, I was continually assigned high-visibility projects, which meant one of the responsibilities was to get other people on board. On board with the change the company was implementing. On board with the new system or tooling to use. On board with a new way of engaging and improving quality of life for our employees. And although the goal was for more people to be able to talk about and encourage others to actively engage and participate, I was typically the one having conversations with those who needed help buying into the idea because other individuals couldn't reach them.

I came to realize what I was doing as a consultant—and again with each project at my new company—was selling.

With each of these projects, I could see the possibilities and knew deep in my heart the difference it would make for my people. Whether it was working one-on-one with my consulting clients or as a project manager/advisor for the 20,000 employees at my last company, I saw each person as part of my group. I was enthusiastic and passionate about something that would make things better for them. Whether it was a successful data transition, implementing a new system, or recognizing people for their accomplishments, each one created better quality of life and provided employees more time doing what they loved, while reducing stress and overwhelm.

It's only since I've been an entrepreneur that I started to view sales differently. Selling is helping by providing books, services, encouragement, strategies, and support that enable others to achieve more of what they want. Selling is an exchange of value for value, where both parties feel safe and abundant. And what's even more important is to not shy away from it but embrace selling as an extension of serving.

Consider this perspective: When you pitch a podcast host to guest appear on their show, you are selling. When you reach out to a school librarian asking for a possible author visit, you are selling. When you have a table at an event with your books available for purchase, you are selling. Even if you're not specifically saying "I have this for sale," when you are providing value, you're selling your brand and what you can provide others.

This starts with remembering your worth and that what you created is of value to someone else. If you go into your business or any appearance opportunity with the mindset of "this is a hobby" or "you can't make money doing what you love," then you'll project this energy and attitude. Desperation can set in as you conduct business because you'll feel like you have to over-deliver to justify being paid.

To unpack what's happening so you can start acting in a different way, grab some paper and a pencil and write your answers to these questions:

- How do you feel about money in general?
- How do you feel about earning money?
- How do you feel about charging for your products and services?
- How did you feel about your first experience earning money?
- What would it feel like if you were receiving steady royalties every month?
- What would it feel like if you were able to pay yourself every month or quarter with plenty of room for business growth?
- What would it feel like if you raised your fees?
- What would it feel like if you had a wait-list full of client work or speaking engagements?

If you can identify past situations where you learned or observed that selling was icky or "you can't make money as a creative," you can also determine how you can change this perception. Going through this exercise may bring up some mixed feelings, but it's worth doing to get you to a space where you can confidently quote the prices you charge. You can say how much a book is at an event without flinching or sounding like it's up for negotiation. You can come through your speaker negotiations with ease and reach the best decision for you. And if you decide not to charge for appearing or presenting at certain events, like speaking at a library or nonprofit, this doesn't mean you're shifting how you see your value. Instead, you reached your decision based upon your goals and desire to support their efforts.

Remember: You are a creative, *and* your creations are valuable. The time, resources, and energy you spent to write your book and get it out into the world matter.

Reflection Questions

- How would you describe your relationship with money and sales?

- What is one thing you can do to improve your relationship with money and sales?

- When was the last time you celebrated a financial win in your business?

- What can you apply from your most recent financial win as you move forward?

- When was the last time you evaluated your services, rates, and prices?

- How confident and comfortable are you in communicating the current prices and rates in your business?

CHAPTER 5

How to Discern the Right Opportunities for You

Simply because you are reading this book, you know you need to get visible to share your book and message. It's not enough to hit publish, even though that is a huge milestone and should be celebrated. Getting your message out into the world is like a marathon because you have to keep showing up and doing the work so you can plant, nurture, and harvest as many seeds as you're able.

Whether you've been asked to be a podcast guest or present at an event, or if you have identified an opportunity you think you would like to be a part of, you will want to get clear if it is truly the right appearance for you to invest your time, energy, and possibly money toward. In the beginning, you'll be excited to do as many as you can, but you will reach a point where you need to pivot and be more selective. If you've reached this point now, or you want to hone your evaluation skills, let the following questions be your guide:

- What was your first instinct when you learned of this opportunity?
- What is the show or event about?
- Who does this show or event serve?

- What is the show or event format?
- Why does this show or event resonate with you?
- Why do you want to be an active participant with this show or event?
- What value can you bring to this show or event?
- Are you comfortable with your brand being associated with the show's and the host's brand?
- Are you excited to attend the show or event?
- Will you be willing to share the show or event with your audience and promote it?
- If there is a cost involved in having a booth at the show or event, is it financially wise for you at the moment, as an investment toward the future of your business or as a profit-making venture?

These questions tie into those from Chapter 1 because they are in direct support of your *why*. When you read the above questions, what else would you add? When you ask any of these questions of yourself and don't pass judgment on the responses, you'll get clearer on what you want more of and what you don't. You'll be better able to position yourself to potential hosts because they will understand what's in it for them. Each opportunity is not only a vehicle to get visible and share your message, but also hone your decision-making, communication, and positioning skills.

There will be times when you know, beyond a shadow of a doubt, you are supposed to do that event. When this happens, trust your instincts and move forward, even if you don't have it all figured out. You will rise up to the next level in order to excel at that event. And on the opposite side of things, there will be times when you are just as confident you need to pass, for whatever reason. And whether it's a firm "no" or "not now," honor what is right for you.

When you run into situations where your decision can go either way, consider journaling to flesh out your thoughts or create a pros and cons list so you can see what's coming up for you and how you feel about it. Make the decision to "act as if" that's the direction you want, then see how that sits with you. Conversely, how would you feel if you didn't attend and were not a part of the event? Sleep on it and see how you feel the next day.

If you say "yes" to this opportunity, go in with an attitude of possibility and joy. Show you want to be there by being on time (or early), smiling, and being ready to engage. If the opportunity doesn't go the way you'd hoped, determine what you can learn from it and move forward. Keep putting yourself out there because the right opportunities will present themselves, and you'll be ready for them.

Reflection Questions

- What type of appearances do you love doing? Why?

- What type of appearances do you least enjoy doing? Why?

- Are there additional questions you can ask yourself to discern the right opportunities?

CHAPTER 6
How to Think About Any Appearance or Event

Depending on how you approach each opportunity, it can feel transactional. Someone purchases a book, and that's it. You guest appear on a podcast, and the magic you've felt in other interviews didn't happen on this interview. Perhaps you do a school visit or another type of speaking engagement, and when you get to your car, you realize the relationship with the host has served its purpose for you both. All that's left is to resolve any outstanding details, like collecting payment or delivering post-event items.

Transactional exchanges and activities do expedite things and focus on the must-haves to complete the exchange. There's nothing wrong with them.

Yet I believe you are reading this book because you want to create a connection with your audience and event host. I believe you want people to have a memorable and enjoyable experience when they work with you, purchase from you, or hear your message. I believe you want to create a *transformative experience.*

My recommendation is to treat each opportunity as a gift to showcase what you are about and why your message is important, which includes thinking about the before and after experiences, not just what happens during the appearance or event. When you make this shift, you'll show up ready to own your space at the table—be seen and heard.

Remember:

1. View any kind of appearance or opportunity as a stage, just in different forms.
2. View each one as an asset to your business.

When it's clear you want to create the best experience for your guests—from the moment they hear about your event until after they've left—your energy and intentionality will radiate and plant new opportunities. These new opportunities may show up during the current event, like book sales or new contacts for future opportunities, or they can occur afterward. It's the ripple effect you create by being thoughtful and intentional with each interaction and engagement.

Yet, sometimes, how to get started can feel overwhelming, when you know you want to create a wonderful experience but aren't sure how.

So, let's start with something you more than likely have done on many occasions in your personal life—hosting an event at your home or another venue. No matter if it's having a few friends over or a huge party or holiday gathering or something in between, you might start with questions like these:

- What do I want to achieve by having this event?
- Why is this event important to me?
- Where am I going to host this event?
- Will it be indoor or outdoor?
- Do I need to make a reservation or not?
- Whom do I invite?
- How will I invite my guests?
- What type of setup will I need?
- What kind of activities will be going on? Music? Games? Movie?
- Are there any special considerations I need to find

out, like food allergies or sensitivities, so everyone invited feels welcome?

- What details would make it feel extra special? Balloons or certain décor?
- Do I want my guests to leave with a party favor?

Completing all these seemingly little things are really the big things that create a beautiful, enjoyable, and memorable event. It's the same skills and thought processes that go into business events, yet those questions might look like:

- Why did you say "yes" to this opportunity, even if you initiated it?
- What message do you want your opportunity to convey?
- What would success look like at this or because of this event?
- Are your customers (adults) and readers (possibly children) the same, or could they be different audiences?
- How will you let people know about the event?
- What type of event is it?
- Where will the event be held?
- Is it a ticketed event, so guests pay to attend?
- Is there a certain dress code?

Let's start with the first question: Why did you say "yes" to this opportunity, even if you initiated it?

Plenty of opportunities will cross your path, and although you may say "yes" to almost each one at the beginning of your business, you'll become more selective through experience and clarity of your vision. When you said "yes" to this event, there was an automatic "no" to other opportunities because those would dilute your energy, attention, or time from this one. As you shift into saying "no" more often, it's important to remember both answers are right, depending on your goals and current season of life.

The common denominator, regardless of which decision you make, is that you are clear on how this event serves your business. Perhaps you've got a new book, and you're looking for as many opportunities to get visible with it as possible. Perhaps, instead of attending many smaller events, you are more focused on a few genre-specific events, holiday expos, and other larger-scaled opportunities. Knowing why you said "yes" is important as you consider the time you will spend preparing for, attending, and doing the post-event work.

When you think about the message you want your opportunity to convey, what comes to mind? We will get into the specifics for book signings, podcast interviews, and speaking engagements in subsequent chapters, but this question is about how you want your guests to feel because they engaged with you. If you're excited to be there, your guests will feel excited and open to engage with you. If you look like you want to be there because you are dressed appropriately and you've done your best to present your business professionally, you'll be taken more seriously. And on the flip side, if you seem bored or tired or your space appears haphazardly thrown together, you'll send a message to your guests that they are imposing if they decide to approach you.

The next thing to clarify for yourself is what success will look like because you were there. For instance, do you want to build a great relationship with the host so future opportunities with them or referral work is possible? How many books sold will feel successful to you? What about connections you make that lead to other guest appearances, like school visits, speaking engagements, or clients for your business? Taking the time to determine what success looks like to you shifts your thinking and the energy you're putting into the event.

Each business appearance you say "yes" to is an opportunity to delight both customers and readers. Going back to hosting an event in your home, if both adults and children were in attendance, you would make sure there were foods, drinks, and activities that each group could enjoy. The same thought process applies with your professional event. And just like those at your home, you may have gatherings that are focused only on one group. When you view each opportunity as a gift to showcase what you are about and why your message is important, you'll identify the best ways to delight your audience.

You'll also want to let people know about the upcoming appearance. This is where your newsletter and your preferred social media platforms come into play. Use these resources to talk about what you have coming up, what you've done, and what you enjoyed. Create events, and invite people when the public can attend—versus a private organization hosting you, like a school visit. Let your enthusiasm come through because it plants the seed for more of them. And if you encounter unpleasantness on your page or in-person, do your best to rise above it. Don't respond or be drawn into arguments. It is a reflection upon the other person, not you.

Lastly, if it's a holiday or themed event, do you need something special to bring the festivities into your space? If the event will be held indoors, will the host provide the supporting equipment you need? If the event is outdoors, do you have the right equipment to protect your work from the weather if it's windy or rainy? If it's a ticketed event and you have friends or family stopping by to give you a quick break, do you need to secure vendor badges or make other arrangements for them to enter?

When you are guest appearing on someone else's stage or space, it's the same idea as if you are a guest at someone else's party or staying in their home. You'd be clear why this event is important to you and focus on bringing your best self. You'd want to know what is expected of you as a guest so you not just meet those expectations, but exceed them. You'd want to leave a great impression so you are welcomed back to a future event.

You are taking the first steps to have a beautiful and memorable experience for yourself and your attendees just by shifting how you think of an event. When you shift your focus and see it as an opportunity to add incredible value, serve generously, and honor who you are, you'll show up to the event with an attitude of gratitude, and that goodness will be returned to you.

Reflection Questions

- What was the last event you hosted at your home? What helped you to feel it was successful?

- Are your customers different from your actual readers? If so, how?

- What comes up for you when you think about getting more visible with speaking events? Book signings? Podcast interviews?

- If different feelings come up for different types of events, which event feels the most exciting to do? Why?

- Which event feels the scariest to do? Why?

- What would help you feel more confident about hosting and participating in these events?

CHAPTER 7

Business and Legal Considerations

One hat you know and wear well is your creative author hat. It's the one where you flourish and is the most comfortable to you, even when you're facing craft-related challenges. This chapter is about the business and legal side of things for an author and business owner and to encourage you to get used to wearing this hat as proudly as you do your creative one.

This chapter may feel like it's covering components that are out of your comfort zone. I felt that way at first, even with an MBA. But I focused my attention on the big picture of running a successful business, which to me includes being business-savvy and legally protected. Making sure my books, my digital space, my intellectual property, and my voice are all protected as best I can provides peace of mind. It doesn't mean I have all the answers when situations present themselves, but it does mean I have the confidence to navigate them with the right team members guiding me.

And I want that for you.

Business License

As a business owner, more than likely you have already established your business entity and secured a business license in your state. If not, visit your local chamber of commerce and work with a tax person you know, like, and trust to complete the steps needed before you start selling. If you will be doing business in a different city or county, look into that jurisdiction's requirements so you are prepared ahead of the event. This same logic applies if your event will be out of your state (or country). Your tax person is your greatest ally when it comes to navigating what you need to do to ensure a smooth process for handling sales and taxes properly in your business, so be willing to ask them for help.

Infrastructure for Selling

If you are going to sell your books directly, whether it's at book signings or through your website, you will want to get a retail sales tax license for your state so you can file the sales tax owed. I recommend taking the sales tax into account when you set the price for your books. Make sure your payment processor is set up to provide receipts and your company's purchase terms. Just like when you purchase an item at your favorite store and the receipt lists their refund policy, this is what I mean by purchase terms. It is something you will want to have, and a lawyer can help.

To handle your inventory management, I recommend either working with a bookkeeper directly or developing a tracking system that also computes sales tax owed so you know how much it is and can make sure it's paid on time. For additional insights on inventory management, read Chapter 13.

For bookstore events, if the host will process your book sales, you'll want to determine with them how payment will be facilitated and by what date. Some events require vendors to provide a raffle item in order to participate, so at those events, keep track of the books you sell versus what you raffled (donated) as that will affect your sales tax owed.

For guest appearances where your fee includes providing books for attendees, confirm with your tax person how to handle the sales tax for those books.

Having established spreadsheets or a recording system will help immensely if you are selling directly in different states and countries—even from local county to county sometimes—which will all have their own tax amounts and details to keep straight.

Professional Liability Insurance

Another way to protect your business is to carry professional liability insurance. In short, this protects you and your business from claims related to mistakes—alleged or not—made by your company. Talk with your tax person or lawyer to determine if this is right for you based on the services you provide and the topics you cover.

To Incorporate or Not?

As an author, you probably started out as a sole proprietor, which means it's just you paying personal income tax on profit earned, and your business is not incorporated. Whether you choose to incorporate as an S corporation or a Limited Liability Corporation (LLC) is a decision you want to make with your tax person and lawyer guiding you. One way you can prepare for this discussion is to map out your business goals and where you see yourself professionally, including the services you provide and if you will bring employees into your business. The conversations you have with your tax and legal team members will provide the best guidance and outcomes for you and your household.

Independent Contractors

There is a difference between employees and independent contractors, and you want to make sure that any individuals you involve in your business or work you do for others spells out the nature of the type of relationship you have. When you have proposed work agreements to review, make sure the relationship between you and the other party is clear, and let your lawyer guide you.

Collect Email the Right Way

Since you'll be meeting new people, events are a great way to build your email community. The key is to know the correct ways to receive email addresses into your business because of various data laws. For instance, if someone emails you directly, that doesn't mean they want to join your email community or get your newsletters. If you add them to your email list without their permission, it disregards what they want, creates a negative impression of your business, and could violate data laws in their location. Instead, offer them an invitation to join your email community, and tell them what they'll get out of it.

Be sure to use an email marketing system that enables you to collect email addresses, honor opt-in rules, send bulk emails (like your newsletter), track email analytics, and provide a way for subscribers to unsubscribe if they so choose. By using an email marketing system, you are able to have direct contact with your readers because they voluntarily signed up to hear from you in a way that honors you and them.

When you use an electronic method for people to sign up, including a QR code for in-person events, you'll be able to not only honor those data laws more effectively, but also provide your lead magnet (a free gift of some kind) to them as a thank you for signing up. If you run into questions, your email marketing system provider will have some resources to help, in addition to your legal resource or lawyer.

Legal Infrastructure - Website

Another key piece to protect your business and honor data laws is to have all of the correct notices linked in your website footer. These notices keep you and your customer or subscriber on the same page, so both of you know the rules. When you are collecting names and or emails, you need a privacy policy, and more than likely, you probably have one on your website. Yet there are several other notices that support and protect your business: terms of use, disclaimers, disclosures, the Digital Millennium Copyright Act (DMCA), and a cookie policy.

As tempting as it might be to "borrow" what you see on someone else's website, I implore you to resist and get your own created. Your website notices, along with any other terms or agreements you have for your business, should reflect what you are doing. If you borrow someone else's, even if they seem really close, there's a chance you could add liability to your business where you shouldn't, or you might omit something you really do need. Work with your legal resource or lawyer to determine the correct notices you need for your business, then create a landing page for each notice and add each page to the footer of your website.

Legal Infrastructure – Agreement Tips for Book Signings

Depending on the hosting organization and type of event, you may or may not have an agreement to sign to have a book signing. In addition to making sure you and the host are on the same page for event logistics, rescheduling or cancellation needs, and marketing efforts, make sure you are clear and agree with any vendor stipulations they may have. Some may require you to have your own liability insurance. Some may require a raffle donation or a portion of your sales to be donated to their overall efforts. Make sure you read all paperwork and agree with them if you want to participate in that event. Be sure to keep a copy of those terms for your records.

Legal Infrastructure –
Agreement Tips for Podcast Guesting

When you're doing more guest appearances, you want to make sure appropriate agreements are in place to protect what you share, what can be done with what you share, and what happens if things go poorly. As host of *The TufFish Show*, I have a guest-contributor agreement that each guest must agree to before coming on my show. It tells them what to expect with their interview, how I will use the content they provide (including their headshot, website links, and bio), what happens if there's copyright infringement on their part, and that no money will be exchanged for their appearance on the show. If you want to be on a show and the host doesn't have an agreement, work with your lawyer to draft one you can send.

Legal Infrastructure –
Agreement Tips for Speaking Engagements

The same can be said for speaking engagements. You want to clearly spell out the details of what will happen for your event. Here are some questions for your consideration:

- What does the service you are providing entail, such as one 60-minute presentation or six 30-minute sessions?

- If there is travel involved, how will that be handled?

- What happens if someone needs to cancel or reschedule?

- How do your books fit into this event?

- Is it okay for the host of the event to take pictures? Will they share with you for your promotional efforts? How else are they allowed to use those images?

- Is it okay for the host to record your talk? Are there limitations on what they can do with that recording?

- How will payment be facilitated? By check, third-party processor, or direct bank deposit?
- When will payment be due?
- If it's a ticketed event, will the host cover your ticket so you can attend other talks?

Let's break these down a bit more. Your agreement should clearly address how long the event itself is and how long your presentation(s) will be. For example, if it's a one-day event that starts at 8:30 am, ends at 5:00 pm, and is followed by a dinner from 6:00 pm to 8:00 pm, your agreement should state the entire duration you are expected to be there. If you are expected to attend the dinner, is that cost covered? It should also delineate your presentation(s) duration and window. So back to the above example: If you are slated to talk for six 30-minute sessions, you want the agreement to spell out when the six sessions will be held so you and your host are aligned.

If the event is out of your area, your agreement should spell out how your travel arrangements will be handled and what will happen if they are not. For instance, perhaps the host will reserve and pay for a hotel room for you, then provide you the details a week or so before your arrival. Or maybe the fee you and the host agree to covers travel, lodging, parking, and food, but you are making the arrangements and paying for those expenses out of the fee received. Make sure you and the host are on the same page in case arrangements that were needed ahead of time were not done. Do you cover the unexpected costs and invoice the host? Is there an inconvenience fee? Although you can't control flight delays, overbooked hotels, or lost luggage, if you are both on the same page upfront, you will have a better way to navigate the unexpected issues.

More than likely, your books support the topic of your speaking engagement. If you and your host agree to provide a copy of your book to each attendee, the cost to print and ship the books should be included in your fee. If you and your host agree for you to have a table at the event where you can sell your books, your agreement should state that the royalties made from this event go to you. How and when to ship books to the event ahead of time should be spelled out, if that's necessary based on your travel plans. If you're donating door prizes or other copies of your books, that should also be clearly stated.

If you have supporting material to design, print, and ship for the event, these costs should be included in your fee. For instance, if you're hosting a workshop and have a workbook to provide each attendee, the print cost for the workbooks should be part of your consideration as you negotiate the fee.

With the additional items you may be printing and shipping, you and the host need to agree what is to happen if the event is cancelled, but money was spent. For instance, perhaps the host will pay for the books, and you'll deliver them. Or perhaps if you had printing costs for supporting material, like a workbook, and your event is cancelled, you accept that it's a sunk cost for this event. If that happens, it just means you have readily available material for the next time you present this content, which could be for this host at another day and time. In your agreement, make it easy for you and the host to reschedule if something happens to the original date.

Since this event is a wonderful growth opportunity for you and your host, you want to spell out how your image, likeness, and content can be used. If the host takes pictures or records your presentation, do you want them to share with you and give you permission to use on your website or add to your media kit? Can they use the images and recordings in other ways? As you and your host identify what supports both of your needs, spell out each of these items in your agreement.

When you think about these costs to support your event, remember to include your speaking honorarium. This reflects the amount paid to you for your time and effort to not only be at the event, but to prepare and practice your presentation.

Each event will look different for these costs. You may decide to waive the honorarium if other aspects of the event make it a valuable use of your time. Weigh each aspect of this event with what it will take to execute it, then put those requirements into your agreement. Itemize any costs, what the host is covering, as well as how and when payment is due so it's clear to you and the host. When you are both on the same page and these details are worked out at the beginning, you'll have a much smoother process.

Speaking engagements and podcasts are a great way to get more visible, share your message to a larger group, and possibly gain new leads. The host is aware of this; however, they may request for you not to "sell from the stage." What this means is that the host wants you to provide immense value to their attendees versus pushing your products and services because you have their undivided attention. You can add a condition in the agreement that says you may invite attendees to contact you or have a slide at the end of your presentation with your website and other contact information. Focus your time and energy on delivering exceptional value, and you'll find this will do more to attract and retain the right readers, clients, and customers because they'll come looking for you.

Final Thoughts

As I mentioned at the start of this chapter, I am not an accountant or a lawyer, so I'm not speaking as an expert in either of these fields. Instead, I am a business owner who values my legal and financial team members and wants that security for you. I know you have what it takes to run a successful business while getting your books and message out into the world simply because you're reading this book. My recommendation is to set aside an hour or so each day to work on your business, and take it a step at a time. Find a tax person and a legal resource (or lawyer) you know, like, and trust, and work with them to navigate each situation. When you view these resources as vital team members—the same as a cover designer or editor—you'll make decisions that help you move forward confidently.

Reflection Questions

- Do you have a legal resource to help you develop terms, website notices, and agreements to protect your business and set up clear rules with customers?

- Do you have a bookkeeping or tax person to help you navigate this side of your business with ease, timeliness, and accuracy?

- Do your purchase terms support the sales in your business?

- Have you reviewed the terms you do have to ensure they are still accurate and appropriate?

- How are you accounting for your book sales tax?

- Do you have a process in place to make things smooth with your inventory and book sales? More on this in Chapter 13.

CHAPTER 8
Mastering Your Style

When you get ready in the morning, do you just throw on anything clean, or do you take time to thoughtfully pull your look together? Do you iron or steam pieces so they look even better wrinkle-free, or do you skip this part because it's an extra step? Does the idea of letting go of clothes that no longer really work for your body type or the direction you're going in your business make you feel excited to update your wardrobe by bringing it into alignment with where you currently are, or does that seem like one more thing to do?

Your clothes—your style—is the first impression anyone gets. When you dress in a way that makes you feel good on the outside, it amplifies the goodness happening on the inside. It shows you value and respect yourself because you take care of yourself.

It's a form of self-care.

When I discovered my favorite store, I loved how polished, organized, and enticing the space felt. The clothes were arranged beautifully, and as I collected items to try on, I couldn't wait to get to the dressing room.

The best part about this store is the people. I vividly remember one of the assistant managers helping me pull together various items to style some outfits. This was the first time I had experienced this kind of shopping. Usually, I would find items, try them on, purchase what I wanted, and put back what I didn't with minimal involvement from store associates.

This store was intentionally different. For instance, they refer to their sales associates as "stylists." As I worked with my stylist, he asked questions to understand what type of business or career I had and what I wanted out of my wardrobe. Armed with this information, he guided me to what really worked for my body type and why.

He chose some items I'd overlooked, but with his nudging, I tried them on and was pleasantly surprised. With each new piece, no matter who picked the item out, I would pause to feel my body's first reaction.

- Did I light up?
- Did I feel excited and confident to wear this item?
- Did I feel heavy or uncomfortable?
- Did I feel a hesitation or scrunch up my face, as though I wasn't one-hundred-percent on board?

His ability to explain why each piece worked (or not) provided clarification to my first reaction. I remember this particular top I wanted to try had all the elements he said to consider, namely texture, color, shine, and interest. This top was a gorgeous purple (definitely my color) and had the other three elements, including a fun, bold print. As soon as I entered the store and told him about the top, he shook his head and said that's not going to work well. When I asked why, he said, although it did have all four elements, he was confident it would look matronly on me. To help me decide for myself, I went ahead and tried it on. Ugh! He was right; it was not becoming on me, so it wasn't purchased. The next item I tried on was a V-neck dolman sweater in the same purple, and I felt fabulous in it. This one was a keeper.

If you need help, line up a styling experience at a store where you love the clothes and trust someone there to show you what really works for you and educate you on why. Or if you'd prefer, ask a trusted friend to go with you. The more information you can share about your event, the event environment, your overall style and goals, the more the stylist or trusted friend will be able to support you. You might consider bringing this stylist or your friend into your home and going through your existing closet. It's not just about buying new pieces, but better leveraging the pieces you have.

Two resources I've found helpful are social media and YouTube because those individuals who excel at this skill will post videos or tutorials for tips. If you find a few people you relate to, like how they explain things, and feel what they suggest works well for you, include those individuals as part of your styling team. Even when you are working from home and using Zoom, you'll want options that make you feel confident virtually, as well as when you have in-person events.

It's easy to think of styling as what clothes to wear, but this also includes hairstyle and/or makeup. Is your current hairstyle showcasing your best features and playing to the strengths of your hair, or is it possible it needs to be updated? As I've gotten older, my hair texture has changed from having a lot of fine hair to fine and thin hair. What worked for me when I was younger, like wearing it around my shoulder blades, now doesn't look becoming on me. Instead, I have found shorter hairstyles suit not only my hair but my personality even more, so letting go of an outdated look and five inches of hair elevated my style and, more importantly, my confidence. Finding some styles and cuts I liked while talking out my concerns and goals with my hairdresser did the same thing as working with my clothing stylist. We also took things slowly so I could ease into what ultimately would work well for me.

The way I view makeup is that it should enhance your natural beauty. It should add to you feeling polished and confident, not take away. If you need some assistance figuring out your best look, or if it's been a while since you've had a makeover, ask for help. Schedule some time with a makeup artist at your local beauty store—or a trusted friend who wears makeup in a way you like—so you get an idea of what would elevate your everyday look to one for guest appearances. Depending upon whom you decide to work with, you may be able to take the makeup you currently have and see what they would recommend for the look you're going for. YouTube and social media video tutorials are also great resources to help you determine colors and the right techniques. Choose two or three individuals that you resonate with, and be open to experimenting with what you have in your makeup bag. When you've got a look you think you like, find some natural lighting and take a selfie to see if you still love what you've created. If not, experiment and try again.

My favorite feature on myself are my eyes, so I focus on enhancing the beauty I see to draw attention to them. If you wear glasses, like I do, make sure the artist or your friend shows you how to do your makeup with and without your glasses on. Be sure to use proper lighting. If you enjoyed the experience and loved the results, consider working with this person again before a big event. And be sure to take care of your skin because it is the foundation.

Here are eleven ways to ensure you are exuding confidence with your style:

1. Choose colors that complement your complexion.

2. Choose clothes that fit appropriately and flatter your body type.

3. Consider the rules of proportion and see if tucking in your top, even just a little bit, or adding a belt creates a more flattering look.

4. Ensure you have the correct undergarments for the outfit and that they fit appropriately; these foundational pieces help the outer pieces lie beautifully.

5. Choose accessories, jewelry, and completer pieces (like a jacket or cardigan) that accentuate your outfit and the occasion.

6. Consider dressing in layers you can comfortably add or remove because facility temperatures can vary greatly.

7. Choose shoes that are comfortable to wear for ten to fourteen hours, occasion appropriate, and not scuffed or too worn.

8. Choose styles that accentuate your personal brand while aligning with your role as a business owner.

9. Choose items in the store when you have a sense of enthusiasm and feel like you could shout "I look amazing" because that's when you know you'll wear them outside of the store.

10. Choose a hairdresser who listens to your desires, clearly communicates, and does a fabulous job with your hair so you'll want to keep a recurring appointment.

11. Practice your makeup look for when you have guest appearances so you confidently accentuate your best features.

Lastly, be willing to donate clothes and accessories that no longer work for you, no matter the reason. Even if the item fits perfectly, but you don't feel like a rock star in it, it needs to move on to someone else. Be sure to throw out expired makeup so what you are using is not only complementing your features, but also keeping your skin healthy. Honor the person you are becoming—the leader you are stepping into.

As you make these styling transformations, it's not just your closet or makeup bag content that will change, but your attitude and presence along with it. You'll find you carry yourself as though you want to be seen and taken seriously.

Reflection Questions

- Does my current wardrobe still work for where I am and where I want to go?

- Do I have pieces that need to be thrown away or donated because I've outgrown them or they just don't work?

- Are there pieces I need to update?

- Would an updated hairstyle feel more aligned to where I am now?

- Does my makeup kit need to be refreshed, including throwing out what's expired?

- Does my skin care routine need to be refreshed?

CHAPTER 9

Detach from the Outcome

Wonderful! You said "yes" to this upcoming event because you felt like it was right for you, and you're full of optimism for what will happen. This enthusiasm, even if it has some butterflies mixed in, is a driving force behind your efforts to prepare and promote this event.

You're excited for the possibilities, as you should be.

But as soon as you are able, detach from the outcome and view this event as an opportunity to plant seeds.

Remember where it started: *Why* do you want to attend or host this event? The reason this clarity is so important is because it shapes your mindset and energy.

When you are in the "I'm glad to be here!" or "It's going to be a lot of fun!" headspace, this positive energy will come through in how you prepare, engage, and present yourself.

The same can be said for the opposite.

If you are telling yourself "I wish I was somewhere else" or "This is so boring," then that will come through too.

There's a big difference between *wanting* to do something and *having* to do something, so choose events you *want* to attend.

And when you are there, no matter how the event plays out, be present. Be engaged. Remember, you chose to spend your time and energy at this event before you knew what the outcome would be, so keep your intention focused on the fact you wanted to be there and trust you will gain something.

I have done many book signings where someone has made a purchase and then it has turned into several school visits or speaking engagements. However, I don't know how many events I've done that didn't go the way I initially expected. I remember one event at which only one gentleman came and purchased a book during the entire three-hour window at that cafe.

I was thankful he came simply because he told me all about his niece. I could feel how much this little girl meant to him. A few months later, at another signing in a different city, his sister and niece came, and the little girl told me her uncle got this book for her as she picked up the title he'd purchased. Then she asked her mom for another title in the series, and as we finished the purchase, her mom told me about how they sought me out because of the experience her brother had with my business. Since then, the mom and daughter have come to a dozen or more events, and each time they both catch me up on what they have been doing and what they are reading.

Seeds were planted at that first event, even though it felt like a disappointment at the time.

On another occasion, I held an event at a local bakery in a prime shopping area. An older child stopped by my table and told me how much she liked my books, but they were below her reading level. I loved that she shared that with me. I commended her accomplishment and asked what she was currently reading, which turned into a lovely conversation about books. The girl encouraged her mom to get my books for a specific child in their family, but her mom decided not to make a purchase. Before they left, the girl returned to my table with a mini hand sanitizer from one of the bath stores and gifted it to me, saying, "This is for you." Be still, my heart! This was over seven years ago at the time of this writing, and I still have it because it was from her. It's a gentle reminder that you don't know the impression and impact you'll have.

One of the best ways I've found to detach from the outcome is to send a heartfelt thank you note to the host organization. A sincere thank you email will go a long way. And if you really want to take it to the next level, find some stationery you love that represents your brand well and send a handwritten note. By taking a few minutes to let them know you appreciate their willingness to either have you as part of their event or provide the space for you to host your own, you are continuing to build your relationships and set your business apart from the crowd.

Each appearance is an opportunity for you to get comfortable with being visible, talking about your message, and trusting the right seeds are being planted, even when it doesn't seem like it at the time.

Reflection Questions

- Why did you say "yes" to this event?
- What expectations do you have for this event?
- What will help you get into the best headspace possible?
- What is your plan to bounce back if this event doesn't go the way you hope?
- What positive things or lessons learned happened because you attended this event?
- How can you detach from the outcome before the event begins and after it takes place?

CHAPTER 10
Let's Talk Book Signings

Book signings offer a wonderful vehicle for you to get visible. They create the perfect opportunity for you to be in the public, with your books, making connections. So, let this chapter be your guide on the tactical considerations for your first or next book signing.

To start, let's go back to what kind of event you are attending to accomplish this signing. Is this at a local eatery or bookstore for a couple of hours? Is it an all-day craft fair? Is it a multi-day expo? Is it in conjunction with a speaking engagement? The type and size of the event will help to determine the quantity of books, swag (giveaways or promotional materials), and other items you need to bring, but it will also help set the tone. To aid in this part of your preparation, read Chapter 6. Then to help you best present yourself as part of the overall package, read Chapter 8.

Let's go through the tactical aspects of your book signing so you're ready before the event and know what to do while you're there.

Table and Tablecloths

The first step is to confirm if you need to bring your own table and chair. Typically, the event host will provide that information upfront, but if you don't know, ask. If you do need to bring your own table and chair, my recommendation is to have a comfortable, cushioned folding chair and either a 4-foot length rectangular table for smaller spaces or a 6-foot length table (also called an event table) for larger spaces. One that folds in half is perfect for easy storage and transport.

Whether you brought your table or are using one the host provides, you'll want to finish it with an appropriately fitted tablecloth that also complements your brand. If you use different sized tables, make sure you have tablecloths that work well with each table. For instance, have one or two regular tablecloths that would support a 6-seat table and an event tablecloth to fully cover a 6-foot table. That way, you have options. If you're unsure what will work when the host provides your table and are unable to visit the site ahead of time to see for yourself, bring several tablecloths so you can adapt. If you have a themed tablecloth that does not touch the floor, I recommend layering it on top of one that does, treating it like a runner. Make sure the covering will touch the floor in the front and on the sides to cover up anything you have stored underneath. Many events specifically require this. If you'll be outside, bring some large clips or clamps to secure the cloth to the table legs so it doesn't billow or blow around.

I saw a social media post with the author sitting behind a table with a few books neatly lying on top, and the caption encouraging people to stop by. Although I couldn't tell the name of the books or what the genre was, one thing jumped out to me.

There wasn't a tablecloth.

Was this the end of the world? No.

Yet, to me, it's a subtle nuance that elevates your table and space because it is a finishing touch.

Depending on your genre, event type, or location, you can use the tablecloth to play off those details. For instance, when I've done book signings for my Einstein and Moo series, sometimes I'll use both a black tablecloth and a white tablecloth to play off the fact that Einstein and Moo are tuxedo kitties.

Tablecloths are like the jacket or statement jewelry that takes your outfit to the next level. It shows you really care about how you are presenting yourself, your business, and your brand.

Displaying Your Books

Now that your table is ready, how do you want to display your books? If you have one or two titles, consider an individual book rack for each one so the books stand up with ease. My first book signing was for the release of *Einstein and the Leaf*, book one in the Einstein and Moo series. To play off the leaf concept, I used a metal picture frame with a leaf on the front to enable the book to stand upright. Getting creative to include some height on your table, whether it's with a frame or a wire rack or something else, creates dimension and interest within your space. It also presents the book cover to guests walking by and helps capture their attention.

There's a picture of Einstein and Moo at three and half months old, on their adoption day, I use as part of my display. My kitties inspired my stories because of the joy they bring our family. To me, I'd be remiss to not show a real-life picture of them. This picture does two things:

1. demonstrates the books are based on real kitties
2. creates a conversation piece at the table.

Sometimes people approach my table because they see the picture and want to tell me about their animals, even if their pets are over the rainbow bridge. Sometimes it's to help a young child make the connection that the picture is of cats, and those cats are the stars of the books. Each interaction is an opportunity to create a connection.

Promotional Banners

Another way to elevate your table or booth space is with a banner—something that displays who you are and what you're about. It should have your name on it, even if you choose to focus on a book or series. Along with the banner, you'll need either safety pins, a poster display stand, or S hooks to display your banner depending upon its size, how it's designed, and the space in which you're working. You'll also want a way to carry your banner to keep it neat and clean.

When the space is just enough for the table itself, I affix my banner with safety pins to the front of the tablecloth. If it's a 10' x 10' booth, like you'd see at an expo, I use S hooks to hang the banner from the curtain rod at the back that is separating my booth from the one directly behind me. By hanging the banner, it's easier for attendees to quickly understand from a distance what my booth is about and where it's located.

Take some time to set up your banner at home, so you know what you need to bring and how to assemble it without the stress of an event starting.

Customers and Readers

Although each book signing will have different attendees due to the location and occasion, the customers at these events may not be your ideal readers. For example, my Einstein and Moo series was written for young children learning to read. The stories have rhyming words and illustrations to help children understand what they are reading. Therefore, when I have these books available at book signings, the adult is my customer, who will ultimately make the purchase, but that doesn't mean my reader, the child, won't be with them. I want my space to feel inviting to both audiences. To welcome children into my space, I hand out bookmarks with the kitties on them, whether or not books are purchased. And when I'm at an event where I can facilitate a drawing contest or story time for the kids, I do. As you think about your customers and readers, consider how you can create a memorable experience for both audiences. Although they will have different reasons for engaging with you, they will come away with the same positive experience because of your efforts to include both.

Bookmarks

Bookmarks add a little something to the purchasing experience for your customer because it's the finishing touch for the item. They also act as reminders of the experience with you. I like to hand out bookmarks, regardless of a purchase. It's a small gesture I can give while detaching from the outcome. If your book is available digitally or on audio, a takeaway like a bookmark with a QR code on it can remind the shopper to look for your book later and buy it the way they prefer. If it leads to additional purchases, someone joining my email community, or reaching out to discuss a possible speaking opportunity, those are exciting results. If it leads to the recipient happily using the bookmark with another book, that's a good thing because they are using their gift. My intention is about sharing a love of reading and joy with someone else. Remember, you never know the ripple effect you'll have.

Gift Bags

Gift bags are a wonderful way to elevate your customer's purchasing experience. I love shopping in boutiques because of the attention to detail they provide. It feels special and intentional, from the items available for purchase to how those items are given to me when I'm ready to leave. For my children's book-related events, I use white gift bags with paw print stickers vertically placed on the front, as though a cat is walking over the bag. And when the books are for the child at the signing, a huge smile spreads across their face as I hand them their special gift bag.

When you think about how you want to handle purchases, consider what you can do to make it easier for the customer while creating a delightful experience. Could you get gift bags in one of your company's brand colors? What about stickers with your logo or something else relating to your books and business? Pay attention to the experiences you appreciate so you can create something special within your business while letting your creativity be your guide.

Handling Payments

Payment processors like Square and PayPal tend to have stickers you can use to show what kind of payments you accept, so determine a way you can display this information. It can be as simple as laying the sticker on the table facing the customer. Be sure to test your equipment before each event, especially if you haven't used it in a while. You may need to update software or charge your processing receivers, and it is better to do those things when you are at home or in a hotel ahead of your event in case you do have faulty equipment to replace or need to determine a workaround. For longer events, pack a backup charger and the corresponding connection cords for your phone and payment processor in case you need to recharge either one during the event and you're not near an electrical outlet.

Final Details

Bring a couple of working pens, updated business cards, a zip pouch to process cash payments (along with enough change options to last through the event), and a few copies of your media kit or one-sheeter to give to those who are considering you for a speaking engagement. If you have other services you want to showcase at the event, design a 4" x 6" to 4" x 9" promotional piece in your brand colors with that information, including your logo and website. These are called rack cards because you typically display them on a rack, so choose a sturdy cardstock. Set up a QR code to your lead magnet or newsletter, and design a flyer you can print and display on your table to build your email community while honoring data laws.

Lastly, arrive at the event with enough time to be set up

and ready to go a minimum of fifteen minutes ahead of the event time. When I think of setup, it includes your table and/ or booth display, checking your payment collection devices, stowing and concealing all transportation and storage equipment, and most importantly, getting yourself centered. It's the perfect time to freshen up in the restroom or refill your drink (with a sealable lid). If it's an event where you can set up the day before, set up your infrastructure, including display racks, so what's left the morning of the event is to add what will go on top of the table.

If the event is out of your area, make your travel arrangements early and allow plenty of time to get to your destination. When you're able to take your time traveling to your event and setting up your space, you won't feel frazzled when logistical hiccups or interruptions happen.

Transporting Materials

If you are responsible for getting your books to the event, a wheeled suitcase does a great job, and using corrugated cardboard or plastic tubs (especially if the event is outdoors) provides structure and sturdiness for the books. They also help to keep the titles separated and organized. A four-wheel wagon or hand truck is also effective. Even if you're at an event where your books will already be there, what else do you need to bring to complete your table or booth? The idea here is to figure out the best way for you to move all of your supporting material in the most efficient, protected, and organized way. One last tip: Have something to protect your suitcase, banner, or contents on a hand truck or in a wagon in case you are moving your books and/or material during inclement weather.

Setting Up Your Event Space

When you think about setting up your space, it depends on the size of the footprint you have been given or purchased. You'll want to use a table that isn't too small or too large for the space, but rather complements it. For example, a 6-foot event table will handle a 10' x 10' space well to present your books and material. However, that same 6-foot table will overpower a smaller space and potentially bump up against neighboring tables.

If you're in a booth, move the table into your space about a foot or so from the edge of the booth entrance, rather than positioning it right at the edge. By situating the table this way, you're inviting people to come into your space and not get caught in the aisle traffic, as well as visually filling the booth footprint a little more. If you're at an outdoor event, bring your own 10' x 10' tent with sides to create your booth and protect your books and material.

Table Arrangement

Now that your table is dressed and positioned well, think about how you like to shop and what arrangements catch your eye so you can bring those elements into your space. For instance, I like the visual of some "white space" so items are easily seen and not crowding each other. I also appreciate varying heights, so I typically use a tall book rack on the corner of the table, then use the rest of the table to arrange and space out other items.

As you're thinking through how you want to set up the table, remember to consider how the person coming into your space will take in your table or booth. You need to factor in two perspectives:

1. How you can easily facilitate transactions from behind the table.

2. How inviting it is for the customer who sees it.

For instance, I put copies of my media kit or flyers on the side of my table opposite my tall book rack. This does two things:

1. groups like material

2. allows items that do not immediately need my involvement to be accessible so I can keep my focus on the customers who are actively engaging with me or purchasing books

And depending on the table size and amount of space, you may not be able to use everything you brought. When this happens, you want to make sure you choose the best pieces to maximize your presence in that space, such that it feels complete and easy to work with for your customer and you.

To aid in your design, use these questions as additional prompts:

- How do you like to see books displayed?

- How do you like to see tables arranged to showcase a variety of items?

- Have you looked at your table from all angles to ensure it works for your customer and for you?

- Does it feel crowded, like there's too much on the table, or scant, like there's not enough?

- Is your conversation piece (like my kitty photo) situated in a pleasing way?

- Are the transportation and storage materials you used visible from the front and sides of the table, or are they concealed with ease?

If it would be less stressful for you to assemble your banner and work through these questions ahead of setting up at the event itself, test your display in your home. It will give you a chance to answer these questions for yourself and make some adjustments so you feel more confident going into the event, even if you make design changes when you're there.

What to Do While You're There

Your table or booth is ready to go, so now what?

If you're at an event where there are more tables or booths and there's time before your event starts, walk around to get a feel for the overall event, as well as how each business is displaying their material. For those you really like, think about how you can bring that element or experience into your own space.

When the event has officially started, even though you have a chair available, stand behind the table. It creates a stronger presence for your space and shows you want to be there, especially when you relax your shoulders, hold your head up high, and smile. Use your chair when you need to sign your books or for a quick break, but then stand up again because when you're standing, you're owning your space. You're more visible and welcoming.

One of the most important things you can do during your event is to stay focused and let your enthusiasm for being there come through by how you present yourself. When people approach your booth or table, offer a friendly greeting, and then give them space to check out your books. When you get the feeling you can engage in conversation, do so with the intent to get to know the other person, not push your books. Consider how you like to be treated when you're the customer, and apply that thought process to how you treat your customers. Whether someone purchases at that event or not, make it your goal to create a wonderful experience while they're engaging with you.

As tempting as it might be to use your phone to entertain yourself when things are slow, please don't as that will create the impression you don't want to be there and are energetically closed for business. And for those potential customers who do approach your table, they may feel like they're interrupting you, which definitely is not what you want to communicate. Treat your phone as a tool to promote your business, whether it is to process sales or promote you are at the event. It is a valuable tool you pull out when you need to use it, then put away when you don't.

Be certain to take a picture of your space so you can post about it on your favorite platforms and use it for when you apply to juried events. Many of those will require photos of your booth at past events. The potential hosts want to evaluate your products, as well as your display, to ensure it's the right fit. Use these pictures as a way to serve your current event and future opportunities.

And if the event is not going the way you want, or it doesn't have the customer foot traffic you had hoped, resist the urge to look at your phone and read or check email. Instead, use it to do a live from the event and invite people to come.

If you're participating at an all-day event, you'll want to stay hydrated and have a few snacks that are not messy to eat and quick to put away when someone approaches your table. I recommend bringing a gallon of bottled water and keeping it under your table so you can refill your lidded cup as often as you need. As for your drink itself, keep it on the floor and in reach of your chair, but not close enough to get knocked over when you adjust or stand up. To protect your books as well as clean your fingers, have some wet wipes or hand sanitizer available for when you eat something and need to quickly clean up. Use slow times to handle restroom breaks, and be sure to take your personal belongings and zip pouch with you.

Lastly, for multi-day events where you're planning to leave your table up, drape an extra tablecloth or top sheet over your display before you leave for the night to protect your table from any dust or dirt and communicate you are not there. On event days like this, I'll set extra business cards on the table before I leave, as well as check my inventory count to determine what needs to be restocked for the following day. If I do need to replenish my inventory, I'll bring the suitcase home so I can reload and move those items with ease. Each night, I'll bring my payment processors with me so I can recharge them, along with my money zip pouch.

Reflection Questions

- When you face your table as a customer, do you like the way the display looks?

- Is it comfortable to work with when you're behind the table facilitating sales and signings?

- If not, what adjustments do you need to make so it feels good for you and for your customers to want to approach and engage with your table?

- Are you excited about how this display showcases your books, brand, and business, or are there some final touches to consider?

- Has my business or brand changed in such a way that modifications are needed to better reflect where I am now?

- How might you improve or streamline your preparation process?

- Did you send a thank you note to the host for having you?

Book Signing Checklist

- Be clear why you want to do this book signing.
- Ensure the host's event agreement terms are acceptable before you start preparing.
- Know the logistics, including type of event, location, date, event duration, set up needs, and attire.
- Make any necessary travel arrangements for out-of-town events.
- Promptly provide the host your bio, headshot, and any other requests they have.
- Think through the optimum way to present yourself and your display to create the best experience possible for your attendees, including pre- and post-event.
- Keep clear communication with your host.
- Allow plenty of time for designing, printing, and shipping bookmarks, business cards, media kits, rack cards, or any other item you want for the attendees.
- Bring business cards, rack cards, media kits, and bookmarks so attendees can connect with you after the event.
- Allow for plenty of travel and setup time. Remember, you are augmenting the host's desire to serve the attendees for that event.
- Trust you are in a space where the host and the host's attendees are interested in you.
- Send a thank you note to your host the following day or as soon as you return home from your event.
- Leverage social media and your newsletter appropriately.

Book Signing Packing Checklist

General

- Table—use the best one for the space: a small rectangular card table or a 6' event table
- Chair—use the best one for the event: a cushioned folding chair, a chair with a separate cushion, or an outdoor chair
- Transportation method: suitcase, plastic tubs, 4-wheeled wagon or hand truck
- Tablecloths that fit your table appropriately, hang to the floor, and complement your brand
- Pens—have a couple, and make sure they work
- Bookmarks
- Rack cards, if desired
- Business cards, including a QR code to your website or opt-in
- QR code flyer
- Media kit or one-sheeter handouts
- Individual book racks and/or tall multiple-book rack
- Conversation piece
- Banner(s) and protective sleeve(s)
- Safety pins, poster display stands, and S hooks
- Cash and a zip pouch
- Payment processors that are fully charged with software updated
- Hand sanitizer and/or wet wipes
- Something to protect your suitcase, banner, or contents on a hand truck or in a wagon during inclement weather

- Your business license and any other appropriate documentation needed to conduct business in the event's city
- Something for purchases, like gift bags

For All-day and Multi-day Events

- Fully charged backup charger and corresponding connection cords for your phone and payment processor
- A gallon of bottled water and lidded cup
- Snacks or meals for the duration that you can eat neatly and quickly put away
- An extra tablecloth or top sheet to drape over your table at night when you're planning to leave your display intact

For Outdoor Events

- 10' x 10' tent with sides and appropriate weights for security
- Clamps to secure your tablecloth
- Sun protection: sunblock, sunglasses, sunhat
- Inclement weather plan:
- Tarp(s)
- Ziplocks the size of your books to protect them/plastic tubs
- Raincoat

CHAPTER 11

Let's Talk Podcasts

Another way to get visible and share your message is through guest podcasting. If you're considering adding speaking engagements into your overall business strategy, podcasts are a way for you to ease into them.

The best way to prepare for a podcast is to make sure you have vetted the show to know how you would provide exceptional value to the host's listeners, and that you would be happy to promote it.

Even though you want to promote your books, business, and brand, if you focus on this during your podcast interview, it can have the opposite effect of what you want. When you focus on being of service to the host and the host's listeners and deliver incredible value, you will attract the right people into your world, create a wonderful asset for your speaking portfolio, and build a great relationship with the host.

To determine if a particular podcast is a good one for you to pitch, listen to some of the episodes first and evaluate it with the below questions:

- Does the podcast host have guests?
- Do you resonate with the topics?
- Do you like the show's format?
- How would you describe the show's listeners?

- How would the listeners connect with your book, message, or business?

- Do you like how the host handles interviews?

- Does the host ask their guests different questions, or is there something you've noticed they ask every time?

Even if you've received an invitation from a podcast host to guest on their show, I recommend you use the above questions to make sure it's still a good fit for you. It needs to be a "yes" for both of you.

If it's not a good fit, what didn't feel right? There's no wrong answer here. If it didn't feel right for you or your brand, you did the right thing by not moving forward. If you start to notice a pattern of what doesn't feel right, it will help you to close the door faster as you move toward more of what you do want.

When it is a good fit and you move forward, go into the interview believing the host genuinely wants you there and the audience will be excited to hear from you. You're going into a friendly space, so trust you will do a wonderful job. The wisdom and information you share will be exactly what this audience needs to hear. When you go into your interview with this mindset, it will relieve some pressure and feel more inviting.

As you set up for the interview, go into it as though it will be distributed through video in addition to audio. Below are eleven tips to run through ahead of your interview to get yourself and your space ready:

1. Drink some water ahead of the conversation to help minimize any coughing or dryness, which could affect your voice. Keep some handy for during the interview.

2. Practice the answer to "Tell us a little about yourself."

3. Practice the answer to "How can people connect with you?"

4. Invest in non-glare glasses if you need them.

5. Make sure the physical space around you and in range of the camera is clean and neat.

6. Avoid using a background filter that can make your outline or hair appear odd as you move around during the interview.

7. Pick a quiet location with no distractions that would cause you to get sidetracked during the interview.

8. Close your email and put your phone on airplane mode so notifications are not interrupting or distracting you or your host.

9. Consider if you need additional lighting, like a ring light, to make sure you can be seen clearly, and test ahead of time to determine the best position for it.

10. Test your technology, like your microphone and earphones, so you can make any adjustments on your end ahead of time.

11. Test your complete setup with the camera you intend to use to ensure you like how you and your space will be shown.

Just as it is important to get the technology and space right, take this care and consideration for yourself too.

One of the keys, I believe, in shining as a podcast guest is to protect your energy ahead of the interview. Sometimes this looks like blocking your calendar with some padding before and after the interview so you can get centered ahead of time and allow for any unforeseen delays afterward. Sometimes this looks like going for a walk, listening to your favorite playlist, or taking your time to get ready so you bring your best self. Perhaps it's a combination of any or all of the above. For additional tips on how to best present yourself so your confidence clearly comes through during your interview, check out Chapter 8.

As I mentioned earlier in this chapter, go into each interview with the attitude that the host and the guests are a warm audience who are excited to have you and for whom you can't wait to provide exceptional value. One easy way to start on the right foot is to smile. You can hear when someone is smiling with what they're saying, as well as through their inflection and tone. It will also help you shake off any nervous energy because your smile shows you're happy to be there. A genuine smile is powerful, and if it feels a little silly at first, remember all the work you have done to get this book out and to this point.

When it's clear the host is wrapping up and you are asked to share any final thoughts, focus on the one thing you really want the audience to remember about their time with you and reiterate that. When the host asks about how the audience can get your book or stay connected with you, share this information clearly and spell out anything that could be confusing to the listener. Lastly, during the recording be sure to thank the host for having you, no matter how the actual interview went.

After your episode has been recorded, send your host a thank you note and tell them what you really enjoyed. Even if it didn't go as well as you would have liked, do your best to find something positive. If you loved the experience, go the extra mile and post a review on your favorite listening app. Periodically share the show with your audience, even if it's not your episode.

When you get the details about your episode, actively participate in promoting it and the show. Add it to your press kit and on your website. Share it with your email community. Each podcast episode is an asset to your business, so go back and periodically share each episode. To keep it fresh, talk about it from different angles, but be sure to recirculate it. When you proudly share your interviews, it demonstrates your interview skills and your eagerness to talk about your work.

Your willingness to get visible and continue to put yourself in the spotlight helps more of your ideal readers and connections discover you. For instance, because you were a fabulous guest on Show A, the host from Show B decided to reach out to you because they knew Host A or listened to Show A. Or someone who is in a decision-making role in their company heard your episode, your message really connected with them, and this person reached out for a possible speaking opportunity.

When you view each podcast interview, each guest appearance, as an asset, you treat it differently. You show up differently. That difference will set you apart from the crowd and cause you to shine as a podcast guest.

Reflection Questions

- Have you done your homework to be a well-prepared and engaged guest?
- Do you have a system in place to keep track of your interviews so you can promote them more than just at the time it airs?
- How can you apply what worked well or didn't work well for you from your most recent interview?
- Did you send a thank you note to the host for having you?

Podcast Guest Checklist

- Be clear on why you want to be on this show.

- Be clear who the audience is.

- Listen to the show before agreeing to be a guest to make sure it resonates with you and why, even if you receive a pitch from the host.

- If you're pitching the host, show you have done your research and share how you can be of service to the host's audience.

- Ensure the guest appearance agreement terms are acceptable before you start preparing.

- Know the logistics, including location, date, interview duration, and attire.

- Promptly provide the host your bio, headshot, links, and any other requests they have.

- Keep clear communication with your host.

- If you receive the interview questions in advance, practice your answers so they sound natural.

- Practice the answer to "Tell us a little about yourself."

- Practice the answer to "Where can we find you?"

- Have your website and media page updated (then update them after you get your interview links).

- Check the technology ahead of the interview.

- Treat your interview as an asset to showcase your communication skills, personality, books, message, and business.

- Make sure your physical background is clean and neat and represents you well.

- Come to the interview as though it will be recorded for video and audio.

- Avoid using a background filter.

- Trust you are in a space where the host and the host's audience are interested in you.

- Send a thank you note to your host shortly after your interview.

- Promote your episode in your newsletter and on your social media platforms, linking or tagging your host.

- Add your episode to your promotion plan to recirculate with your email community and on your social media platforms.

CHAPTER 12

Let's Talk
Speaking Engagements

Whether it's a school visit, workshop, summit session, or keynote—virtual or in-person—these are all speaking engagements. And they are great ways to connect your message with your ideal audience. When your audience hears your voice talking with them on a topic that brings you joy and serves them well, magic happens.

Now this may seem over the top, to say "magic happens," but in my experience, it's true. I have spoken to thousands of elementary school children about the Einstein and Moo series and owning their uniqueness, and each time, without fail, children come up to hug me and tell me about their animals and their dreams. When I have had multi-day events at schools, children who I engaged with on day one find me on day two to share the book they wrote and illustrated when they got home the night before. Parents have approached me months, even years, after I've visited their child's school, telling me how their child still remembers me and the positive impact of our time together. Each time I've done a speaking engagement with adults as my audience, I receive similar feedback. People come up and say it was exactly what they needed to hear, or they email well after our time together to tell me of the progress they've made.

You can have this kind of ripple effect with your speaking engagements, so let's get started.

Vision and Topic

As you might have guessed, the best place to start is to know how this speaking engagement serves your business. Just like with book signings, plenty of opportunities will cross your path, so why did you say "yes" to this event? The vision for your business provides an umbrella that your speaking engagement supports, so take a few minutes now to reread Chapter 1.

Next, brainstorm your answer to this question, and write down what comes to you: How do you view your role as a speaker? For instance, are you a guide? An encourager? A teacher? A subject matter expert? More than likely, several of these will resonate with you and aid in how you put your presentation or speech together and how you handle yourself during the presentation. Having clarity of your vision and role as a speaker will make your preparation easier and more enjoyable because you're clear on your why, your audience, your role, and how this event will serve your business.

The topic for this speaking engagement needs to support your overall vision and connect with the attending audience. You probably have several topics you'd love to share with your ideal audience and readers, so take a few minutes and write them down. Get clear on how they align and support your overall vision. If you are part of someone else's overall event by way of providing a workshop, a session, or as the keynote speaker, make sure the topic you are presenting aligns with the host's goals, as well as your own.

As you develop presentations, they can become products you sell within your business. Going back to the school visits I have done, I created the presentation one time, but I've delivered it countless times. When I talk with a decision-maker about a school visit, the presentation is discussed like a product, with features and benefits, so the person hiring me knows what the students and school will get out of doing an author visit with me.

Your Host

Speaking of decision-makers, your speaking engagement has two clients: the person who has hired you and the audience itself. Although you are a guest in the host's space, you augment the host's mission to provide value to their attendees. When the host hired you to be the event speaker or presenter, they extended their credibility to you with their audience. Thus, you not only represent yourself and business, but to some extent, you represent the host. Embrace this role by dressing one step above the expected attire for guests at the event. Show up early so you and your host have plenty of time to set up before welcoming your attendees. Stay after the last attendee leaves to break down what you brought, as well as offer any support to the host.

Your Audience

As with any opportunity where you are getting visible with your message, ask yourself: Who is the intended audience, and why are they there? By learning more about your attendees, you'll be able to hone your presentation to serve them. And those attendees who resonated the most with your message will more than likely take the next step with you, such as joining your email community or purchasing something from you. As you think about the attendees specific to this presentation, grab a piece of paper and a pencil and answer the following questions:

- What do you want them to *feel* because they attended your event?
- What do you want them to *do* as a result of attending your event?

As you brainstorm your answers, allow anything and everything that comes up to be included. Nothing is too small or too big. If it seems too big, try breaking it down into smaller chunks. The intent here is to have a clear idea of your desired outcomes for this appearance, then work backward to create a presentation and any supporting pre- and post-event infrastructure to support your goals.

Speaking Agreement

When you think about the infrastructure you need to facilitate a wonderful experience, part of this involves using an agreement that will create the boundaries of what you and your host expect within the space of this event. It is important for you to clearly spell out the details so you both are on the same page. If you need a place to start, check out Chapter 7 for some questions you'll want to have addressed within your agreement. If your host provides one for you to review and sign, make sure those terms are acceptable before you start preparing. If they are not, for whatever reason, have a conversation with your host to bring the agreement into balance for you both. This event should be a win for you, a win for the host, and a win for the audience. When in doubt, work with a lawyer you know, like, and trust in your state to navigate the agreement.

Presentation Structure

Now that the topic is determined, the audience is clearly understood, and there is an acceptable agreement in place, let me introduce to you the Presentation Sandwich.

A sandwich has layers, and two of the layers typically involve the same item: bread. Whether your sandwich has condiments, cheese, meats, vegetables, or any combination of those, the concept of the sandwich is the same. The first layer is the first slice of bread, add your individual ingredients, and finish with the second slice of bread.

Your bread represents how your topic serves your audience. This is where you connect with your audience, both at the beginning and the end, so they realize you understand them and why this topic matters to them. Your ingredients represent the stories, data, and examples you use to expound upon your topic and make it relatable to your audience. Make sure you are creating correlations between each of your two or three key points and your audience.

Let's say you have three key points to support your overall message. The first slice of bread is about introducing you, your message, your main three points, and most importantly, why it matters to your audience.

Next, treat each point as an individual ingredient. Perhaps for one point you use some data or an analogy. Perhaps another point is an experience you've had that can help the audience. With each point, continue to ensure your audience feels you see them and that they understand what's in it for them. Give them actionable and tangible tips. If you're using a slide deck, let it amplify your message and be a visual prompt for you, versus something you read verbatim. You want the audience to pay attention to the message—not get bogged down or feel like they don't have to listen because the slides have everything.

When you're ready to close your presentation, use the second slice of bread to recap the points you shared in a way that leaves your audience feeling as though what they've heard is possible for them, and you're the right person to help. If you're using a slide deck, put your logo, website, and QR code to your lead magnet on the last slide to make it easy to connect with you.

As you are assembling this sandwich, think about conferences, workshops, or other events you have attended. Usually, there's a lot of excitement and possibility stirring because you're at the event with like-minded people. Then you get back to "the real world," and sometimes it can feel like you had a break, not a breakthrough. With that in mind, do your best to ensure your presentation, workshop, or speech helps the audience get the breakthrough they want because they spent time with you.

Supporting Material

Does your presentation content need supporting material created? For instance, do you need workbooks for your attendees to complete during your time together? How about a "leave behind" that lists the key takeaways or offers some kind of encouragement your attendees can use afterward? Do you need other supporting material, like props, to amplify your message? The intent is to bolster the experience for your attendees.

As I mentioned in Chapter 10, I like to hand out bookmarks, regardless of a purchase, at book signing events because it's a small gesture I can give while detaching from the outcome. I also do this for school visits because it creates a wonderful experience for the children afterward. To do this, I ask my contact ahead of time for the number of students per teacher for the grades scheduled to attend so I can make sure each child receives a bookmark. I'll preassemble the bookmarks in individual envelopes by grade and by teacher, so when those classrooms attend their author visit session, I give the teachers their respective envelopes to distribute. In this way, bookmarks are the supporting material I need for an author visit.

When I have done an event with an activity built in, I make sure the supporting material, such as workbooks, worksheets, pencils, stickies, or visual props/displays, are all identified, purchased, created, or printed ahead of time. For my first corporate speaking engagement, I wanted to create an uplifting experience during our time together, as well as actionable steps for my attendees after the event. To do this, I incorporated a workbook into the presentation that had space for each attendee to identify their next three steps. This meant the workbook was my supporting material and needed to be developed, designed, printed, and shipped.

Earlier in my business, I had booths at various pet expos to sell my books, and some of those times, I was offered the opportunity to give a talk on their entertainment stage. Obviously, I said "yes" and modified my author visit presentation to suit the needs for this talk. In order to draw more attention to my business and books, I hosted a drawing contest at my booth after my talk so the kids could win a prize for the best drawing of Einstein and Moo. With this scenario, drawing paper, crayons, and a prize were the necessary supporting material.

The key with your supporting material is that it should add to—not subtract from or derail—your presentation, so be intentional with your choice of what it is and how you incorporate it.

Event Prep

Just like with a book signing, you need to know the logistics, including type of event, location, date, event duration, presentation duration, travel needs, audio visual (AV) needs, and attire. These details should be articulated in the speaking agreement you signed, so be sure to use that as your guide. If you need tips to master your style, revisit Chapter 8.

If you negotiated for your books to be part of the event in some manner, you'll want to weave those logistics into your overall planning. Whether you negotiated as part of your overall fee for each attendee to receive a copy of your book or to have a table and sell them outright, be sure to place your book order as early as your printer/distributor needs so there is time to print the total quantity, plus ship to your desired location. If your agreement permitted you to have a table and sell your books, revisit Chapter 10 for book signing specifics.

Along the same lines as your books, allow for plenty of time to design, print (or purchase), and ship any supporting materials, including what you would need if you're also going to have a booth or book signing. When you receive these items, take the time to quality-check them. If you're able to do that at your house, great! If you've had them shipped to your destined location, quality-check them there as soon as you're able.

Lastly, your host is your ally, so keep your communication lines open with them. If you run into problems that could be resolved with their help, reach out. If you have AV needs to support your presentation, let your host know. For instance, do you need a projector, internet access, a handheld microphone or one that is clipped to your clothing, or a podium? Be specific with what you plan to use and what connections or cording it may require. If possible, bring options with you to accommodate input/port size differences. Your host may have already shared what they have available for you to use, but if not and you need something, ask.

If your host has deliverable deadlines they need met for promotional purposes or AV testing, get your information to them promptly. Be ahead of schedule. If you are expected to promote the event, do so in a timely and enthusiastic manner. Remember, you said "yes" to this event because you want to be there and felt it was the right fit for you and your business, so promote it with the same excitement you first felt after accepting the offer.

Practice

Your audience, host, and your message deserve your best effort, which means practice. Even if you write out every word you hope to say in order to get all of your thoughts organized when you're first getting started, practice the material enough to move away from any detailed script. Use it as a starting point, but then prepare a few notecards to keep you on track. You'll not only hone your speaking skills, but you'll be so familiar with your content that if you go off script, it will still feel appropriate for the message and audience. During my first corporate speaking engagement, I found myself improvising a bit, yet it felt as though it should have been part of the presentation from the beginning. However, I would not have been able to do that if I hadn't practiced for hours and hours ahead of time.

When you're practicing your presentation, start about a month or so out, gradually adding more time as the event gets closer. When you first start practicing, use the run-throughs to refine your content and time yourself to see how long it takes you to complete the entire presentation. My recommendation is to have a printed copy of your slides or speaking notes and track your timing. Do you reach slide six within the first ten minutes of your presentation, and if so, does that work well for you? If not, do you need to condense some material or rework a couple of slides so you are where you want to be at that point?

Within two or so weeks of the live event, I recommend you practice actively delivering your presentation. In addition to tracking your time, consider how you really would deliver this message. Would you stand up and move around if you had an audience with you? If you would, practice that way. Practice projecting your voice so if someone was in the back of the room, they could hear you. Practice several run-throughs focused on what your body is doing and the tempo of your delivery so you are confident your body language and vocal delivery support your presentation. If you get nervous during the live event, you will probably fall back to how you practiced, so get that muscle memory and confidence level established.

If you are presenting online, practice your delivery sitting in your chair, toward the edge of the seat, fully upright. I recommend recording yourself on video so you can watch it back and check not only the content and delivery, but also your location, lighting, camera placements, microphone, and earphones.

Regarding your location, pick a quiet place with no distractions that would cause you to get sidetracked while you are presenting, including closing your email and putting your phone on airplane mode. Consider incorporating a ring light to enhance your attendees' ability to see you clearly. Just make sure you don't wash yourself out.

Although you can't control what happens live, especially if you're joining someone else's virtual space, you can do your best to be as technologically set as possible. If you are presenting online, make sure the area within the camera's range is neat and on brand so your digital space represents you and your business well.

Your Headspace

As I've mentioned several times in this book, I believe it is important to protect your energy ahead of the event. In order for you to give your best to this event, and especially your presentation, you need to be in the best headspace possible. To offer some insights into what I mean, let me share how I prepare for any event, but especially book signings and speaking engagements.

Leading up to the event itself, I make sure I have all the things I need to bring with me. My checklists help with that, so I use them each time when I pack. If it is a speaking engagement, I will have practiced for several hours each day up to the day before the event.

The night before, I choose my outfit, press any items that need it, unwind with my hubby, say my prayers, and go to bed at a reasonable hour. Sleep is vital.

The morning of, I'll spend some time in prayer and meditation, then review my notes a few times and take my time getting myself together. I'll play one of my favorite energizing playlists and sing to burn energy and warm up my voice. I'll pack my things, including a water bottle, then I'll stop by a Starbucks and get an unsweetened black tea, all the while listening to either my playlist or an uplifting message.

You probably noticed that each of these activities aren't unusual, yet each one adds up to help me get and stay in the best headspace possible.

Take your time to do what works for you to be focused and calm.

What to Do While You're There

Event day is here, and you're set with your presentation and books to the best of your ability. As you look for your host, take time to check out your environment. Your observations will help you adapt to your space. Take some time to chat with other attendees. Just like with book signings and podcast interviews, the four most important things you can do during your event include:

1. Smile

2. Stay hydrated

3. Stay present and let your enthusiasm come through

4. Trust you are in a space where the host and the host's audience are interested in you.

The host would not have hired you and put out the effort needed to bring you in if they did not believe in you. The host wants you to be successful because that means they provided an incredible and valuable event to their attendees. When the host wins, you win, and vice versa.

If you get off track during your presentation, take a moment to collect yourself and resume. Your audience doesn't know what you were going to include. They only know what you've shared thus far. Given that you have accomplished hours and hours of practice, you'll be able to pick up where you need to and move forward. If you skipped something, trust that it wasn't needed at that time. If you improvised and added something that wasn't part of your preparation, trust that it was what this audience needed, and it fit in at the appropriate time in your presentation. You know your material inside and out. If you need to peek at your notes, do that and keep going. And when you're done, thank the host and audience for having you.

Reflection Questions

- Have you done your homework to be a well-prepared and engaging speaker for this event?

- What are some improvements you can garner from your most recent presentation to apply to your next one?

- Did you send a thank you note to the host for having you?

- Did you follow up on any connections made with others at this event?

Speaking Engagement Checklist

- Be clear why you want to do this presentation, workshop, or keynote.

- Ensure the speaker agreement terms are acceptable before you start preparing.

- Know the logistics, including type of event, location, date, event duration, presentation duration, and attire.

- Make any necessary travel arrangements for out-of-town engagements.

- Promptly provide the host your bio, headshot, presentation files, payment forms, and any other requests they have.

- Develop a clear message that will create an experience and provide value for your audience.

- Remember, your speech is a product that must serve two groups—your host and your host's audience—so understand the needs of both.

- Think through the best way to present yourself and your material so you leave the host and your host's audience with the best experience possible, including pre- and post-event.

- Ensure part of your presentation invites the audience to take another step that is outside of the event to continue their experience and growth.

- Practice your presentation by standing up, monitoring your body language and tempo, projecting your voice, testing your technology, and using a stopwatch to track the time.

- Know your AV needs and confirm if you are expected to bring them or if the facility/host will provide them.

- Keep clear communication with your host.

- Allow plenty of time for designing, printing, and shipping any printables, takeaways, rack cards, or workbooks you want for the attendees.

- Bring business cards and leave-behinds so attendees can connect with you after the event.

- Allow for plenty of travel and setup time. Remember, you are augmenting the host's desire to serve the attendees for that event.

- Check the technology ahead of the presentation, including at the event's site.

- Trust you are in a space where the host and the host's audience are interested in you.

- Send a thank you note to your host the following day or as soon as you return home from your presentation.

- Leverage social media and your newsletter appropriately.

CHAPTER 13
Keeping It All Straight

Each appearance requires effort for it go well. Some will require more, some less. Some events may require you to manage your book inventory, in addition to keeping all of the event-related tasks moving and done on time. To compound this situation, when you have multiple events going—with different needs and at different stages in the process—you'll want to have systems and tools in place to help you keep it all straight. Let's work through how to handle these various situations by creating an inventory management process and a project management process.

Inventory Management

In Chapter 7, I mentioned the importance of finding a bookkeeper/tax person. This professional is a valuable member of your team, especially when it comes to understanding your book inventory. Whether it's a book signing or a speaking engagement where you will have books as part of the appearance, you'll want to create a system that will work well for you and your tax person, so identify this professional and involve them in your efforts early.

If your event is at a bookstore, where they are to provide books for you to sign, process the inventory, and provide your portion of the sales, you want to account for that revenue with your tax person on your income statement. It's similar to when you receive your publisher and third-party royalties because it is revenue with no inventory to manage.

If you are responsible for bringing the books you're selling and, therefore, processing the inventory (and possibly payments), there are extra steps. The first step is to have an efficient way to transport your material to your event, and Chapter 10 offers some ideas. Next, you'll want to create an inventory management process to track movement of your books.

When I created mine, I counted every book and organized them by format and title. Although this step may sound tedious, it creates a solid foundation for your inventory management system. If you have copies of hardbacks and paperbacks of the same title, treat them as separate entities and sell them at different price points. I built an Excel spreadsheet to track when books were distributed, how many, and for how much. This same spreadsheet has a formula to calculate the sales tax, so I know at the end of each event how much is owed. Each time I complete an event, I verify my physical inventory numbers and update my Excel file.

You'll need to:

- Set up an accurate income statement
- Set up the proper calculations for inventory costs
- Understand the impact to your costs when you give books away versus sell them
- Set up a process to ensure sales tax is computed accurately and paid on time

Your process may look different than mine, and that's okay. Your bookkeeper/tax professional may recommend another way to handle and track inventory, and as long as it works for both of you, that's good. Remember, this person is a valuable member of your team, so keep the lines of communication open. When in doubt, ask and get their help.

Project Management

When you think of getting all the tasks done for a successful appearance or event, does it feel achievable or overwhelming? Without a system in place, it can easily become overwhelming, especially when tasks for multiple events are due around the same time.

To work through this, I recommend choosing a project management tool you think you'd enjoy using and build several templates. Each template should include every task to be done related to that event. As you refine your processes more, you update the template. This way, you create a rinse and repeat process. Create one template for book signings. Create a second template for when you're a podcast guest. Create a third template for keynote speaking. Create a fourth template for workshops.

Let's take one example to break down. In my project management/task management tool, I have a project called Book Signing Template, and these are the tasks associated with it:

- Add event to website
- Create event on Facebook page
- Announce event in newsletter (and keep until after event)
- Design social media graphics
- Schedule social media posts
- Make sure QR code is set up to opt-in landing page and working to collect new emails
- Print QR code flyer
- Print a copy of press/media kit
- Print business cards and rack cards, if inventory is low
- Pack (see Book Signing Packing Checklist for details)
- Go to bank, get cash for event

- Attend event
- Take pictures of table/booth after setup
- Update inventory
- Go to bank, deposit cash
- Send thank you note to host organization
- Remove from website

As soon as I confirm a book signing will happen, I make a copy of the Book Signing Template, rename it to the event, and assign dates to the individual event tasks. If modifications are needed to that specific event, I'll adjust the tasks accordingly. For instance, if a book signing event is three days instead of one, I'll add tasks to support the extra days. Whether I have one event or ten events overlapping, I know exactly where I am with each one. Once all the tasks are completed for the event, I delete the event-specific project from my app.

For keynotes, school visits, and workshops, I have separate templates for each of them and follow the same logic as with the Book Signing Template. Because these events involve more preparation, I suggest your templates have tasks that support handling the agreement, ensuring the invoice is sent and paid, developing and practicing the presentation or workshop material, developing and printing supporting material, getting the host any requested material by their due dates, and updating your CV.

For guest appearing on podcasts, as you might have guessed, I have a template to help me track:

- When the interview is
- When I need to provide the requested material to the host
- When I should receive the episode graphic and pre-publish links
- When the episode will air

Additionally, I have tasks for updating my CV, drafting my promotional newsletter, scheduling in social media, and setting up the episode for future re-shares. Remember, each appearance is an asset to your business, so make it work for you beyond a "one and done" approach. One way to ensure you recirculate your interviews is to create a spreadsheet where you keep track of each episode share. Another way is to use a social media scheduler that allows you to recirculate with ease after the initial post.

As you are creating and refining your inventory management and project management systems, consider keeping a piece of paper and pencil handy when you are preparing for your next event. Write down each step you are doing and in what order. Use that handwritten list as the start of your checklist, or use what I've provided. Either way, give yourself the grace you need to act, learn what you don't know, speak up when you need help, and give yourself permission to refine your processes as often as you need.

Reflection Questions

- Is your inventory management system set up and working smoothly?

- Is your project management process working well, or are some tweaks needed?

- Is your project management tool working well?

- Do any of your templates need to be adjusted to better reflect what you do?

- Are new templates needed?

- Do you need to update your CV with your latest accomplishments?

- How long has it been since you repurposed any previous interviews?

CHAPTER 14

Celebrate

Congratulations! You have achieved another milestone and accomplishment in your business and along your author journey. By having a book signing event, doing an interview, or leading a speaking engagement, you stepped out of your comfort zone and got visible. You got in front of new people, and some of those individuals purchased your books or signed up for your newsletter. This took courage, and you did it! You moved your business another step forward, which also means progressing to a new level.

So, celebrate the progress! Celebrate your courage and initiative. Celebrate what you gained by doing this appearance.

It's easy to celebrate the big things in our lives, but how about the small steps that really moved the needle? It may sound silly to celebrate those, yet they add up. Sometimes, it's the seemingly smallest step that may be significant and meaningful to you.

In fact, I would like for you to implement JRP into your process.

JRP, pronounced as "jerp," is my affectionate acronym for Jen's Reward Program. It started because I really dislike getting my blood drawn, so after I would have an appointment, I'd go to Starbucks and get my favorite tea as a reward. One thing led to another, and an inside joke was created with several family members indoctrinated into the program. Each person's reward suits what works for them, and I love that. In fact, this is the whole point.

When I've done something that's brave for me, I get a JRP. When I've accomplished a huge milestone, I get a JRP. It doesn't really matter what the JRP is. It matters that the event or step I'm recognizing is meaningful to me, big or small, and is celebrated. Sometimes, it's getting an unsweetened tea from my local Starbucks. Sometimes, it's going to my favorite clothing store and getting a top, or a dress, or a new pair of shoes.

So, I'm curious: Do you celebrate the small successes or only the really big ones? Do you celebrate when you've been brave? Do you plan to celebrate so you look forward to it, or does it happen organically afterward? I ask these questions because I think the longer you're on this author and entrepreneurial journey, the more you need to realize how far you've come. Give yourself the credit you deserve for running this marathon that started the moment you had the idea to write your book.

And just as it's important to celebrate your wins and forward steps, celebrate the rejections. They are redirections that will get you where you're supposed to be. It is more information you now have because you tried that path. Without those setbacks, you wouldn't be where you are, and you are so much further now than when you published your book. If celebrating the rejection feels too much, get curious what you can learn from the rejection and treat it as an opportunity to try something new. The first attempt may not have gone the way you wanted, but by getting curious and trying something different, you redirected your efforts and energy to find a better outcome. When you reframe the rejection in this way, it's a blessing and a step in the right direction, even if it feels backward or sideways.

Reflection Questions

- What was the last step, big or small, that you celebrated?

- What helps you work through rejection or setbacks so you keep putting yourself out there?

- What JRPs can you plan on for your next success?

CHAPTER 15
Post Event

You showed up and did your best for the book signing, podcast interview, or speaking engagement you lined up. You've celebrated, thanked your host, and handled the inventory management and project management aspects your event needed.

So, now what?

A big part of what happens now is what you put in place when you initially started working on this event. What did you want people to do, feel, or believe after leaving your event? Perhaps you wanted them to take the next step with you by signing up to be part of your email community, book a call, purchase a course, or purchase your book. If it was one or more of these actions, be sure to have the digital infrastructure in place to facilitate each of these as effortlessly and efficiently as you can. Perhaps you wanted them to shift their mindsets and try something different. If this is the case, you may never hear about what those shifts or new things are.

Either way, you have done all you can to create the next steps for your attendees to take.

Have faith you planted plenty of seeds. Trust you will nurture your community to the best of your ability so seeds start to take root and grow. Let go of any expectation of *how* and *when,* and focus your time and energy on what you can do. If this is something you find challenging, which can happen for any of us, revisit Chapter 9 as you continue to detach from the outcome.

As you move forward, focus on delivering incredible value with each newsletter you send to your community. Be sure to include a call to action for someone who is ready to take the next step with you. For instance, mention your recent book or your backlist. Share the next workshop you'll be hosting. Tell them about your upcoming initiatives, and invite them to be part of the experience. And if you provide one-on-one services, talk about the next step and the results you've heard and seen from previous clients.

And of course, focus on identifying new opportunities to get visible and share your message. You were courageous with this appearance or event because you got visible, and as such, you've learned a lot from this experience. When you think through your recent opportunity, it's easy to identify where you stumbled or felt ill-prepared, but a lot of things went right. What were they? Take a few minutes, grab a sheet of paper and a pencil, and write out everything that went well, big and small, even if you think it's too small to include. The idea here is to allow your thoughts to flow while silencing your inner critic that can become selective. When you see all the goodness that happened, it will enable you to discover the progress you've made and remind you that you are capable of way more than you might have thought.

Going back to what could have been better, jot down what comes up for you without making it personal. Focus on the process and free flow as you objectively consider what could have been better. If you felt ill-prepared during part of the process, write down what was going on and what you did to cope. If you were as prepared as you could possibly be and something still didn't go the way you wanted, get curious if this is really about the preparation or about adjusting your expectations.

Next, how can you use your constructive evaluation, as well as any constructive feedback you received? If you received stellar feedback and can turn it into a form of social proof, be sure to add it to your website and create appropriate social media posts to showcase your work. If getting help from someone else during your preparation efforts would make a huge difference in how smoothly things come together for you behind the scenes, stay open to figuring out who this could be and how it would work. What do you want to continue to do because it worked well and brought you and your attendees so much joy?

At the heart of the previous questions is this: How can you refine your process to make it even better for you and your attendees for your next opportunity? It doesn't have be big. Baby steps and tweaks are great because you can easily measure the results. And even if you are knocking each opportunity out of the park, remember to stay grounded, realize each one is a gift, and treat it that way.

Each event or appearance opportunity is a chance for you to move to your next level, no matter how big the step is. It's a chance for you to refine and hone your skills and message so you serve your audience well and make the impact you want to have.

Reflection Questions

- How did your last opportunity go?
- What would you love to see happen with future events?
- What didn't go as well as you would have liked?
- What adjustments can you make to improve for the next time?
- What else can you do to nurture the seeds you've planted?
- Have you created a testimonial or feedback loop?
- What helps to keep your mindset in check?

Now What?

What you accomplished took courage, and you have it. And from my standpoint, I know you did a fantastic job! You were willing to get uncomfortable, to be visible, and share your book and message. I am proud of you and excited for you!

Whether this was your first opportunity or your hundredth, each one is a little different and will require something more from you. Each one is a chance to stretch and strengthen your current skills, own your greatness, allow more people to be part of your world, and grow as a creative and business owner.

The *Author Stylist Guide* was created out of love as my pep talk for you. As I've said throughout this book, I believe if the story came to you, you are the right messenger. When you published your book, it started a new phase of your journey. One where you let people know you and your book exist. And even though you might have been talking about your message with your readers and ideal audience before book publication, you need to keep going.

It's a marathon, not a sprint, so go at the pace you need.

Take baby steps and keep going.

And when you need support to elevate your appearance opportunities, let this book:

- Be your back-pocket resource to help your book and message attract the right people for you
- Remind you of the courage and skills, gifts and talents, you already have because without them, you would not have gotten this far

- Remind you what you're capable of so you move to your next level with more ease

- Encourage you to experiment and refine what you do because it's necessary for your growth

- Remind you that with each appearance opportunity you'll learn, grow, and gain more confidence as you build your portfolio and get in front of more people

- Support you stepping into your role as a business owner as you select the right opportunities and own your space each time you show up, present your business, and deliver your message

When you can see how far you've come, you'll feel a sense of joy, excitement, and accomplishment. You faced the unknown, just like you did when you started writing your book, and you made it happen. Even if you were nervous or uncomfortable, you did it, and you have added to the ripple effect for your book and message.

If you know more support would help you excel with your next book signing, interview, or speaking engagement, I'd love for us to chat. When we work together, you can count on me to:

- Ask deep and insightful questions that lead to breakthroughs

- Hold space and provide kind and constructive feedback that brings out your best self

- Provide strategic and practical guidance that makes your next level achievable

Visit https://www.jennifermilius.com to learn more and book a complimentary consult call so we can see what's possible.

Thank you for including me along your journey. I'm honored you chose to spend your time and energy with me and can't wait to hear what you've accomplished.

Keep letting your light shine!

Acknowledgments

It takes a village, as several podcast guests have said on my show, to bring a book to life! And this book is no exception. I am so thankful to have some incredible people in my world who supported and encouraged me to get this book written and shared.

Thank you to my husband, Mark. From supporting my writing time and giving me feedback on each chapter so I could complete this book, thank you. I love you.

Mom and Dad, thank you for believing in me ever since I can remember. Thank you for coming to my events and listening to me talk about my business, including this newest book. I'm so blessed that out of all the parents in the world, I get to call you mine.

For your encouragement, love, and support, I am thankful for my sister friends and cheerleaders: Julia Jones, Tricia Purdy, and Kimberly Smith-Salmon.

Meredith Hancock, thank you for the beautiful cover and interior layout. Our paths crossed ten years ago when you helped me bring my tuxedo kitties, Einstein and Moo, to picture-book life. Thank you for sharing your talents with me once again!

Meg Welch Dendler, thank you for being my fabulous editor, as well as fellow cat lover. Your enthusiasm and keen eye made this manuscript ready for sharing.

Dani Lanzarotta, thank you for your friendship and encouragement, our breakfast strategy sessions, and for being a wonderful sounding board.

Alexa Bigwarfe, thank you for your friendship and for generously sharing your guidance and insights with me so this book could make its way into the world.

Kris Staton and Tamsen Horton, thank you for helping

me make sure I have the proper infrastructure set up in my business and guiding me when new opportunities arise.

And to my trusty furry supervisors—Einstein, Moo, and Cap'n Jack—thank you for sharing my office and my chair while I, er, we worked. Thank you for bringing our family so much joy and love.

About the Author

Jennifer Milius is an entrepreneur, developmental editor, coach, and accomplished multi-genre author who leverages her 20-year corporate career, undergraduate Communications degree, and MBA to help creatives bring out their inner greatness so they get comfortable using their voice, sharing their message, and being visible.

While in corporate, Jen ran oversight for dozens of trade shows, as well as attended hundreds of shows as a booth attendant. She partnered with senior leadership for keynote communications, whether it was developing content or guiding them on how to present that material and present themselves. Since starting her business in August 2014, Jen has hosted over 150 book signings, including booths at multi-day expos. Jen has helped hundreds of authors and creatives move to their next level, whether it is through coaching, developmental editing, refining keynote speeches, instructions through courses or workshops, or even having them on *The TufFish Show.*

Having spoken to thousands of elementary school students about courage and confidence and worked with hundreds of authors and creatives, Jen believes when you share your gifts and message, you bring joy to others and show what's possible for them. Tapping into your full potential means that joy, purpose, and possibility are coming together through you.

Check out her website at www.jennifermilius.com

www.ingramcontent.com/pod-product-compliance
Lightning Source LLC
Chambersburg PA
CBHW071431210326
41597CB00020B/3747